DARWIN ON THE GREEN

DARWIN ON THE GREEN

A Further Collection of the Golf Writings

of

BERNARD DARWIN

SOUVENIR PRESS

First published 1986 by Souvenir Press Ltd,
43 Great Russell Street, London WC1B 3PA
and simultaneously in Canada

ISBN 0 285 62769 4

Photoset by Rowland Phototypesetting Ltd
Bury St Edmunds, Suffolk
Printed in Great Britain by
Billing and Sons Ltd, Worcester

CONTENTS

EDITOR'S NOTE

Bernard Darwin began writing about golf for *Country Life* magazine in 1908 and his last piece did not appear until 1961, shortly before his death at the age of 85. A special lunch was held in honour of the 50th anniversary of his joining the publication. On that occasion it was recalled that, with the exception of the First World War years, when *Country Life* took the view that golf was too frivolous a pursuit to deserve space in such tragic times and Darwin himself was serving as a major in the Army, he had missed only one issue of the magazine. That, it should be said, was not his fault: the liner bringing his copy from the United States in those less technological days was delayed by Atlantic gales.

When Darwin first joined *Country Life*, its golfing coverage, edited by Horace G. Hutchinson, bore the title 'On the Green' and consisted as a rule of short and newsy, if stylishly written, stories about golfing events of the time. There were occasional longer pieces, presumably when there was a shortage of news, but it is not always possible to identify them as Darwin's work—even if one suspects they were —because they carried no by-line. However, there was one, entitled *A Christmas Sermon* and published as early as 1913, that was of the same genus as the urbane, knowledgeable and amusing 'golf commentaries' he wrote after his return from the war whenever there was no championship or other important golfing event to cover. By the time he died, these much-loved and much-admired 'commentaries' exceeded three million words, a treasure house of golfing lore and reminiscence, written in an easy yet elegant style that remained virtually unchanged throughout his long career and set new standards in covering not just the golf scene but other sports as well.

The title *Editor's Note* at the head of these few words is something of a misnomer: Darwin was too good a writer to require editing in the normal sense of the word. The real task was to decide the basis for choosing what to use from his vast output. In selecting the pieces for this book I therefore decided to try to reflect to some extent the story of golf as well as opening the treasure house of Darwin's writing to a new and wider audience.

The best way of achieving both these objectives seemed to be to choose at least one piece, where it was possible to identify him as the author, from each year of his long association with *Country Life*. I have, among others, selected his first by-lined article, written in 1908, which was a dissertation on the varying methods used by distinguished golfers of the period, and his last, recollections of some stormy Championships. How the game was played nearly 80 years ago may seem of remote interest today. Yet several of the points raised in that particular article have their echoes in modern times. Snead, for instance, took the view that golf would be a much easier game if the left side could be got out of the way, and, among the stars of golf today, Trevino, like John H. Taylor all those years ago, favours an open stance. Similarly, whether it is better to stand or crouch when you are putting, a subject exercising Darwin's mind as long ago as 1914, is still the subject of debate today. Much may have changed, but it is clear that, then as now, there was no generally accepted view about the best way of playing golf and any statement on the subject was more likely to cause an argument than a discussion.

H. J. WEAVER

GLOSSARY

Changes in ball design were the chief influence in increasing the popularity of golf between the middle of the nineteenth century and the start of the twentieth. Basically there were three types, all of which make their appearance from time to time in Bernard Darwin's discourses about the game:

The feathery   Dated from the early seventeenth century and was made by stuffing the leather cover with compressed boiled feathers. The feathery could be hit a long way. In wet weather, however, it became waterlogged and was easily damaged by a bad iron shot. Consequently, as featheries were nearly as expensive as a golf club, players relied largely on wooden clubs and rarely carried, for use in emergency, more than one iron. The feathery was superseded in 1848 by—

The gutty   Made from gutta-percha, a product from the gum of trees found in South America and the South Pacific islands.

The earliest gutties did not 'fly' well until they bore the scars of use (the fore-runner of today's familiar dimples). Nevertheless, the gutty was around 80 per cent cheaper than the feathery and virtually indestructible. Hence it enabled thousands to play golf, who had previously been unable to afford the game. Iron clubs became more common and varied. The gutty was superseded in its turn in 1898 by—

The rubber ball   Made of rubber thread wound around a solid rubber core. The rubber ball cost 2s. 6d. (12½p), about half the price of a wooden club, when it was introduced to this country. However, the cost proved unimportant because the ball was so much pleasanter to hit and flew so far (courses had to be lengthened to accommodate it). The result was yet another surge in the popularity of the game.

Golf clubs (the instruments, not the buildings) are nowadays, of course, numbered and standardised. Some of the earlier clubs, which are mentioned regularly, and usually with nostalgia, in Bernard Darwin's Writings, include, with their modern equivalents:

Brassie:	No. 2 wood.
Spoon:	No. 3 or No. 4 wood.
Driving iron (cleek):	No. 1 or No. 2 iron.
Midmashie:	No. 3 iron.

Mashie iron:	No. 4 iron.
Mashie:	No. 5 iron.
Spade mashie:	No. 6 iron.
Mashie-niblick:	No. 7 iron.
Pitching niblick:	No. 8 iron.
Niblick:	No. 9 iron.

Cleek was the general name for an iron club. A *jigger* was another name used for an iron employed for approach shots to the green. A *putting cleek* had a long, shallow face and was like a cleek, but with more loft. It was a boon for putting on rough greens that bore little resemblance to their manicured equivalents today, and for defeating *stymies*—the path to the hole blocked by an opponent's ball—that are no longer part of the modern game.

A QUESTION OF STYLE
(1908)

Apart from the excitement of watching a close finish, which was this year conspicuous by its absence, the amateur spectator at an open championship will derive more amusement from observing how the ball is hit than whither it is hit. This is at all times a difficult task, and is made more so by the annoying fact that there are a large number of other people who are also selfishly bent on seeing the shot played. Indeed, during Braid's last round the crowd was so dense that one thought one's self lucky to see the head of a club or the foot of a champion, and could sympathise with the small children depicted in an ancient *Punch* peeping under the flap of a circus tent to see the ''oofs of the 'osses.' Persistent watching for four days, however, lead to some conclusions, possibly erroneous, as to the features that can and should be imitated in the styles of the great golfing masters. It would be presumptuous to say which is the best, but one may with more propriety form an opinion as to which the humbler player may most safely imitate.

In some there lurk hidden dangers for the unwary. What, for instance, can be more fascinating than Massy's driving? It is the perfection of ease and force combined, and yet who could safely copy the curious little flourish of the club over the player's head? Massy sometimes seems to accentuate it himself, with a slight slice resulting. With the imitator the clubhead would inevitably describe a loop after the manner of a pig's tail, and the result would be indescribable. Golfers are apt to vary in their sentiments as to Taylor's swing. Personally, I find him the most attractive of all players to watch; but he would be a brave man who should set out to model his style on Taylor's. In the first place, he stands very open, though perhaps not quite so pronouncedly as of old, and the ordinary mortal can seldom drive steadily for long together with the right foot much advanced. For a bit all goes well, and then suddenly he finds himself falling on his nose, to exaggerate slightly, in the middle of his swing. The imitator is apt to give a tremendous dig with the right forearm showing a lamentable lack of follow through.

Then, who shall attempt to imitate Vardon's method of taking up the club? It seems to go up so straight and close to the body, and yet with Vardon it looks absolutely easy and natural. If we try to imitate him, we shall develop a great deal of jump and lose all vestiges of swing. Braid seems upon the whole the safest model of these great men. He stands very square to the ball, and will not ensnare us into too open a stance, as Vardon and Taylor might. His swing, too, has plenty of sweep in it, though there must be a great deal of skilfully concealed hit as well to make the ball go such prodigious distances. Braid's club seems, in a way, to come down quite slowly, and yet with terrific force, and this contradictory phenomenon is generally noticeable in the style of the very best players. Looking at all the drivers, I could see no style the imitation of which would lead us into so few pitfalls as Braid's, however puny and paltry might be our reproduction of it.

In the matter of iron and mashie shots, Massy has one conspicuous virtue worthy of our attention, and that is a short but pronounced pause at the top of the swing, which might save us from much moving of the body and hurrying of the stroke. As regards short approaches played with a cut, nearly all professionals provide a lesson to nearly all amateurs. They have a certain deft and well-defined manner of playing them, which few amateurs seem able to emulate. It is a stroke which may be seen played by any small caddie idly pitching his master's ball into a tee-box, but it is, apparently, necessary to have passed through the caddie stage in order to do it properly. It is seen to particular advantage in the chipping of a clean-lying ball out of a bunker. The professional will flick the ball out with apparent ease, when the amateur will, from sheer terror, take a full shot with a niblick and inches of sand behind the ball.

The putting is, as a rule, the least impressive part of the business from the onlooker's point of view, and it is certainly the least impressive part of the game of the great champions of golf. Vardon, indeed, was so sadly off his putting on the first day as to provide an object-lesson of how not to do it. Braid, in his rather curious and artificial style, undoubtedly holed a large number of good putts, and, if he missed one or two very short ones, who shall cast a stone at him? The great merit of Braid's putting style appears to lie in the infinite patience with which he waits for the head of his club. He takes the club back very slowly, so that it appears certain that his hands must come through far too soon and in front of the ball. He manages, however, to keep his left wrist back till the head of the putter has come back to the ball, and for the most part at Prestwick he was timing his putt beautifully.

Many players, Massy for instance, have a prettier and more natural style of putting, but Braid seemed to hole the ball at awkward distances more frequently than any of them. Many of the professionals have followed Braid's example in using an aluminium putter of the 'Braid-Mills' variety. Braid himself stands very upright to his putts, in the manner of one using a wooden putter; but other wielders of the aluminium club putted with it in the same style as they would employ with a cleek, and it was curious to see Herd, a typical Scottish putter with the cleek, crouching and knuckling over with the aluminium club. Most people experience a difficulty in avoiding pulling with these lofted aluminium putters, and Braid seems to get over it by pushing the ball slightly out and away from him.

The ordinary wooden putter did not seem much in favour, though Mr John Ball was temporarily using one, without, however, affording it any conspicuously good advertisement. Indeed, had this ex-champion putted better he would have been very high in the list. The rest of his game was of his very best, and when we are talking of swings to imitate there is still no style more perfect in the whole world of golf than that of the great Hoylake player.

To conclude these rather desultory remarks, there was one lesson to be learnt from watching the best players, and that was to play quickly and avoid a superfluity of waggle. Braid never, at the most critical moment, varies his one solitary waggle with the little pause or flourish in the middle of it. Massy's waggle is so rudimentary and slight as to be practically non-existent, and Duncan is almost quicker even than Massy. Vardon and Taylor, too, cut down preliminaries to an almost irreducible minimum. One prominent exception there is, and that is Herd. His waggles are very attractive, and they are the resolute flourishes of a good player, as unlike as possible to the timid waverings of the bad player who cannot wind himself up to hit the ball; but still there are four and sometimes five or six of them, so that Herd must be put down as the exception which proves the rule laid down.

A GIDDY HARUMPHRODITE
(1909)

Nga Motu has suddenly leapt into fame. Till recently it was, so far as we are aware, as insignificant as was, for example, Rugely before the late Mr William Palmer committed his murders there; now the name of Nga Motu will echo down the ages as having elicited the famous judgment that 'a croquet mallet is not a golf club and is therefore inadmissible.' These are momentous words, and the Rules of Golf Committee may soon be so badgered and brow-beaten and inundated with further questions as to wish the words unsaid. The question addressed was *à propos* of the pronouncement that no substantial departure from the accepted make of golf club will be sanctioned. 'Is it permissible,' it was asked, 'to use a little croquet mallet?'

Now the Rules of Golf Committee have no doubt been actuated by a praiseworthy desire to see golf played as such, and not travestied by horrible ungolf-like weapons wielded in ungolf-like attitudes. That is all very well, but those who disagree with them will have plenty of arguments to show that their weapons are clubs, and they will add that to stop a man getting a ball into hole in the way he likes best (provided, of course, it be a fair stroke) is rather arbitrary and high-handed, and possibly *ultra vires*. If they cannot prove that their weapons are clubs, the malcontents will at

least be able to set the committee a series of 'posers' as to
where to draw the line between a club and a mallet. 'When is
a club not a club?' Answer: 'When it's a mallet.' 'When is a
mallet not a mallet?' Answer: 'When it's a club.' So far that is
thoroughly satisfactory; but, then, let the form of croquet-
mallet putter which is most generally seen be produced
before the committee. What will they make of it?

It is a 'kind of giddy harumphrodite,' putter and mallet,
too. The shaft is the shaft of a club, the grip is the grip of a
club, but the head is the head of a mallet; at least, it is like the
head of a mallet, but infinitely smaller and made of an
entirely different substance—to wit, aluminium. If the test
of the question is whether the thing would be suitable to play
croquet with, then it is not a mallet at all, for it would only
move a croquet ball made in miniature. It is hard to find
any principle in it which can be distinctly said to belong
wholly to croquet. There is, to be sure, the shaft running
into the middle of the head, but that is now no new thing,
since the Schenectady putter has been in common use since
1904. It is hard not to think that the committee have been led
away by a natural distaste for seeing a gentleman putting
between his legs with his hands held in a most inartistic
manner.

To forbid a stroke which, in so far as it is not a push, is a
perfectly fair one, appears analogous to forbidding the
potting of the white ball at billiards, or the pulling a ball
outside the off stump to square leg. It is not, save under
exceptional circumstances, a profitable manœuvre to pot the
white ball, and it used not to be considered profitable to pull
a ball on the off side; from these simple facts there arose
among the muddle-headed an absurd sort of fiction that he
who did either of these two things was guilty of a horrible
and dishonourable action. In the same way, to play with a

grotesque club in a grotesque attitude is not, as a rule, profitable; but to do so is not therefore necessarily unfair, and to declare that it is unfair, which is what the Rules Committee appear to have done, implies some confusion of thought.

THE HONOURABLE COMPANY
(1912)

On three days in next week, and two days in the week after, the open championship will be played for the fifth time in its history upon the links of the Honourable Company of Edinburgh Golfers at Muirfield. To write of Muirfield and the Honourable Company is to mingle the new and the old. It is now twenty years since Mr Hilton won the first championship played at Muirfield; but there is still some suspicion of undue youthfulness attaching to the course. Perhaps because the course really was rather too new when the championship was first moved there, and because, moreover, there were many regrets for the glory which thereupon departed from Musselburgh, Muirfield has never quite recovered from that suspicion, once just, but now unjust. On the other hand, the Honourable Company has a very long and illustrious history, much of which is to be found in Mr Kerr's admirable *Golf Book of the East Lothian*, to which I am much indebted.

It was neither at Muirfield nor at Musselburgh that the members originally played, but on the links of Leith. The first regular minutes belong to the year 1744, and from that time onwards is to be found a regular society carried on with all due formality and decorum, as may be seen from the solemn certificate of admittance of a Mr

Alexander Strachan of Tarrie. Each member had such a certificate, the motto in most cases being 'Far and sure,' and not the more chaste and classical 'Vi et arte' of Mr Strachan.

All sorts and conditions of men played golf over Leith Links and dined at the taverns of Straiton and Luckie Clephan. We have a pleasant picture of them drawn by no less an historian than Smollett, who had pointed out to him 'one particular set of golfers, the youngest of whom was turned four score. They were all gentlemen of independent fortune who had amused themselves with this pastime for the best part of a century, without having ever felt the least alarm from sickness or disgust, and none ever went to bed without having the best part of a gallon of a claret in his belly.'

This was a few years later than 1744, when the first minutes were recorded, and the Council of Edinburgh, in a stately document, presented a silver club to be played for. The club remained the property of the town, and their only liability was to announce the day of competition 'by tuck of drum' and to send the club to Leith to be duly played for. And—which is particularly interesting—the competition was open to any golfer who should send in his name in due season; in fact, something very like a first championship. Twenty years afterwards there were too many golfers on Leith Links, or golfers became less democratic, for the Captain of the Golf admitted only such noblemen or gentlemen as he approved to be members of the society, and only members of the society could compete.

It was stated in the original document that the victor was to be called the Captain of the Golf, and was thereupon to append a gold or silver piece (as he pleased) to the club. This pleasant custom still continues. One club was covered with silver balls by 1811, and the town gave another. This in turn was covered, and the one to which this year Mr Robert Maxwell as captain solemnly appends a silver ball began its career in 1879. It will be seen that the fashion of the ball changes, the old smooth 'featheries' giving way to the 'nicks' and 'pimples' of more modern balls. I do not know if any captain was ever 'pleased' to append a gold ball. It appears that with native prudence they have all been content with silver ones.

After the silver clubs we come to three delightful Company portraits, though by them hangs rather a sad tale. In 1831 the club ceased to play at Leith, and in 1835 it began to play at Musselburgh. Between those years it was in a defunct, or at any rate dormant, condition, and a dreadful thing happened in that the pictures were dispersed.

Raeburn's portrait of 'Singing Jamie Balfour', the former secretary and treasurer to the Company, was bought by a caddie, so it is said, for thirty shillings (£1.50) and sold by him at a modest profit of ten shillings (50p) and two bottles of whisky. However, an excellent print of the portrait (for which, by the way, the artist was paid but thirty pounds) survives in the hall at Muirfield.

Mr Balfour was not only secretary and treasurer to the Company but a gentleman of many talents—musical and convivial. According to Chambers's *Traditions of Edinburgh* he is represented in the picture as singing one of his favourite songs, 'When I ha'e a saxpence under my thoom,' with appropriate action and 'a merriness of countenance justifying the traditionary account of the man.' He was a great singer of Scottish songs, both grave and gay, and a mighty drinker. His taste in beverages seems to have been a thoroughly catholic one, for whenever he heard a bottle opened with a particularly loud and cheerful sound he would call out, 'Lassie, gi'e me a glass o' *that*,' deeming further enquiry unnecessary.

There is a pleasant story told of him that, going home late after a carouse, he tumbled into a pit formed for the foundation of a house. A passer-by, being entreated to help him out, declared that it would be useless, since he would not be able to stand if he were out. 'Very true, perhaps,' said Balfour, 'yet if you help me out I'll run you to the Tron Kirk for a bottle of claret.' He was accordingly picked out, and there and then ran off with so amazing a swiftness as completely to defeat the good Samaritan, who ultimately arrived to find him sitting on the steps of the church, unable to stand. 'Another run to Fortune's for another bottle of claret,' said Balfour, and off he went again, winning the second bottle and ultimately sending his new friend home to bed, quite prostrate in a chair.

He was beloved by the members of the Company, and when he died they mourned his death in a not inappropriate manner. A general meeting was held at Leith, at which all appeared in mourning. Immediately after dinner and the drinking the health of the Company came three toasts. First, 'To the memory of our worthy and late departed friend, Mr James Balfour'; second, 'Comfort and consolation to the friends and relatives of Mr James Balfour'; third, 'May the offices in this society held by Mr Balfour be agreeably supplied and attended to with that accuracy and precision for which he was peculiarly distinguished.' After this 'the Captain proceeded to general toasts.'

The portrait of William St Clair of Roslin, painted by Sir George Chalmers in 1771, went likewise. It now belongs to the Royal Company of Archers, but a replica has been painted and hangs in the hall at Muirfield. This William St

Clair was Captain of the Company and first Master Mason of Scotland.

In this last capacity, and being in 1768 'now in his grand climax of golfing,' he laid the foundation of the clubhouse on Leith Links with three strokes of the mallet. For one who ever reached a grand climax of golfing, his style is certainly a peculiar one. Many of the old pictures show that the 'right foot back' was the ancient rule of orthodox play, and, it was said, 'we never remember to have seen anyone hit so pronouncedly to square leg as Mr St Clair.'

The other gentleman represented in a portrait was Mr James Hay, a very placid and agreeable-looking old golfer, but, as far as I know, not one of any extraordinary fame.

We are apt to have the idea that there was in golf in the eighteenth century one noble and simple rule, 'play the ball where it lies,' and that the modern and degraded practice of 'life and drop' was never thought of. This was not the case.

The *Company's Articles and Laws in Playing at Golf* are signed by Mr John Rattray, who won the silver club on the first occasion of its being played for and was the Captain of the Company in 1744 and again in 1751. They are, as may be observed, exceedingly and delightfully short, but they hardly convince us that a short code of rules is all that is necessary, because it is not hard to see where difficulties of interpretation might have arisen. Is it not, for example, easy to imagine two Lords of Session arguing at great length, and with the most perfect obstinacy, as to what did or did not constitute 'any wattery filth' within the meaning of Rule 5? As may be seen by the postscript to the rules signed by Mr John Boswall, who was Captain in 1858, frequent disputes did arise over this fifth rule, and also over the thirteenth. Whether Mr Boswall made the matter clearer by his new rule would seem to be rather doubtful.

As to Rule 13, it may incidentally be noted that the ball after being lifted and teed was to be played only with an iron club. The rule as to lost ball, again, was much less severe then than it is today. We have to lose the hole if we lose our ball; but in Mr Rattray's time we should have been able under Rule 8 to go back to the spot whence we struck and play another ball, while allowing the adversary one stroke 'for the misfortune.'

Of the Company's medals, the one bearing the design of crossed clubs and a ball, which has somewhat the appearance of an old 'Eclipse' golf ball, is the spring silver medal. It was presented by Sir Walter Simpson, who wrote that most amusing and at the same time depressing manual of golfing philosophy, *The Art of Golf*, and dedicated it to the Honourable Company, 'Humbly as a golfer, proudly as their Captain and gratefully for merry meetings.' The other bears a picture of the grandstand at Musselburgh, in a room at the back of which the members of the Company kept their clubs when they first migrated from Leith.

In the third picture of medals we find mingled ancient and modern history. There is the name of the great Mr W. M. Goddard in 1843, and again thirteen years later, in 1856, next door to that of Mr (afterwards Sir Robert) Hay of Newbyth, who once played him a great match for one hundred pounds and beat him easily, thus vindicating the new school against the old. Later on are to be seen such famous names as those of Dr Argyll Robertson, Mr Robert Clark and Mr Gilbert Mitchell Innes, and so gradually on to Mr J. E. Laidlay, and from Mr Laidlay to this year's Captain, Mr Robert Maxwell.

So much for the ancient glories of the Honourable Company; and now for something of their links today. In the first place, I think personally that Muirfield has never quite had justice done to it. Those who play much golf there are fond of it, but in the general world it is the fashion to speak rather disparagingly of it. Why, I can never quite discover, unless the reason lies in that grey stone wall that surrounds the course. As one stands in front of the clubhouse, one sees the whole course lying before one, neatly walled in and looking worthy of that which was its ancient name, 'the hundred-acre field.' Yet there is a jolly view of the sea and a rather fascinating wood, with its trees all bent and twisted by the wind, and, which is more to the point, some uncommonly difficult golf to be played.

I shall not describe the course at length, but may just add a word or two as to the recent changes. Some of them are real changes, while others consist only in a rearrangement of the order of playing. For the first five holes the course proceeds as of old. Then, instead of turning to the right—I suppose a Scotsman would say to the south—over the big bunker to the old sixth, we keep along the wall due east to the old ninth. Thus the old tenth and eleventh become the new seventh and eighth. The ninth is a hole of the 'dog-leg' order, played from the north of the old eleventh green to the old 'pond,' or seventh green. The new tenth is the old eighth, and thus we come back to the old sixth and duly play it, though it is much longer than it used to be and is now called the eleventh. From this point onwards the round is the same; we have still to steer the ball to those horribly narrow holes, the thirteenth and fifteenth, and must still end with a manful carrying shot over the deep, trench-like bunker at the home hole.

The last two amateur championships that have been played at Muirfield Mr Maxwell has won. It is almost too much to hope for that he should win the open championship, too; but, at least, he should make a good show, for he is just a little bit better at Muirfield than anywhere else, gauging the length of those deceptive iron shots with an ease born of much practice, and being able to putt on the Muirfield greens, which is more than many people can do. It is a course, moreover, of good omen for amateurs, for the first championship that was played on it—in 1892—certainly showed the amateurs in a brighter light than any other championship since. At the end of the first two rounds, Mr Horace Hutchinson was the leader; at the end of the third Mr Ball led, with Mr Hilton second; and at the end of the fourth Mr Hilton was open champion, and Mr Ball, if I remember aright, tied for second place. I am afraid we shall never live to see such another championship as that.

The next championship at Muirfield in 1896 was likewise an historic one, because it provided the first triumph in the career of Harry Vardon. Vardon tied with Taylor, who had already won two years in succession, and beat him on playing off. It is now difficult to imagine Vardon as a nearly unknown player, but he played the last hole of his last round in that championship with but ten people to look at him, and several holes in the middle of the round with no spectators at all. This is on the authority of Mr Hilton, who was his partner for the round.

In 1901 there was another Muirfield championship with another new champion in the form of James Braid, and he won there again in 1906 with the fine score of 300.

There would seem to be no very particular reason why he should not win yet a third time at Muirfield, and a sixth time in all, unless, indeed, the reason take the shape of Vardon, who is also in search of his sixth championship. In the duels between these great men this summer Vardon has so far had something the best of it, and he is certainly playing magnificent golf. We have heard less of his missing short putts since he took to his new putter with its narrow little face, though his method of striking the ball on the green is hardly reassuring. There are many others to be considered also, and any one of them who can average 75 for four rounds over the Muirfield of today should surely have a good chance of being the open champion of 1912.

A CHRISTMAS SERMON
(1913)

A friend who is a recent and zealous convert to the game of
golf has provided me with the text for a sermon which is, on
the face of it, admirably adapted to a season of peace and
good will. Whether a general following of its tenets would, in
fact, be productive of those blessings I am not so sure.
Briefly, my friend complains that golfers are not what Mr
Yellowplush called 'beneviolent'; they never tell him what
he is doing wrong in his shots, nor do they tell each other.
Indeed, he had been so much impressed by this universal
minding of their own business that he had come to believe
that to tell a fellow-golfer of his faults was contrary to the
'etiquette' of the game, a dread code of which he stands very
properly in awe. He declares that, if better players would
more often go out of their way to help worse ones by pointing
out their errors and the appropriate method of amending
them, it would make for the general happiness of the world.

It is always interesting to know how institutions and
societies to which we have been long accustomed strike a
perfectly fresh mind, and there is a good deal in the
contention of my eminently Christian friend. The sad part
of it is that he will probably lose all too soon this first bloom
of benevolence, and a year hence, if I tell him that he appears
to me to be committing some crime or other, he may snarl at

me that it constitutes a deliberately considered part of his
style to which he attributes the successes that have attended
him on all but that particular day.

The undoubted fact is that many of us do not like being
told of our golfing mistakes any more than we do of those we
make in more serious walks of life. We say we do and think
we do, but in truth we very often do not like it at all. I think
this is not wholly on account of extreme sensitiveness or
extreme annoyance. We have so often been given counsel
that did us no good whatever that it makes us both incredu-
lous and irritable. I can remember personally, with profound gratitude, certain pieces of advice, given to me when
my game was in a parlous description, that put me on the
right track at very useful times, but I can remember infinitely
more than consisted of the deadliest truisms. Therefore, as
a general rule, the benevolent person should know something of the game of his victim and should be tolerably
certain that he has something worth saying before he says it.

Most people have a certain delicacy in offering advice
unasked upon any subject, and this is particularly true in
golf. The superior player fears that his doing so may savour
of patronage, the inferior of impudence. Though a mouse
may help a lion, yet, on the whole, the inferior player
exercises a wise discretion in remaining silent, but the
superior should not be too self-consciously afraid of his
motives being misunderstood. Needless to say, he will
conduct himself with ordinary discretion; there are colonels
and generals and other ferocious old gentlemen to be found
on the golf course to whom it would be as much as his life
was worth even to hint a fault. But in the case of milder
persons, so long as he makes some modest preface to his
remarks, he will very likely earn much gratitude and no
resentment.

There is, of course, another reason why the offering of advice is a rather ticklish affair. It is a well known fact that quite admirable golfing instruction which will ultimately bear good fruit may, and often does, for the first moment, reduce the learner to complete impotence. There is, moreover, nothing so disturbing to the right match-playing frame of mind as the trying of experiments in the middle of the game. Therefore, to attempt to coach an adversary is one good way of beating him. I suppose those who have reasonably clear consciences are not afraid of incurring the suspicion of trying deliberately to 'put off' our opponent; but they may be justifiably afraid of achieving the same results with the highest motives.

The more distinguished is the adviser, the greater the weight of his words, and, if a champion says nothing more original than 'Keep your eye on the ball,' we listen reverentially and proceed to look at the ball with so tremendous and concentrated a glare as to preclude all possibility of following through. So the champion who is kind enough to throw a word to us must remember, if he be a conscientious man, that a great responsibility rests upon him. It scarcely matters how nonsensical his advice, if we have confidence in him we shall hit the ball for a while; but when the next bad time comes, as come it must, his lightly spoken word may do great harm, because we shall persist in following it with blind, unquestioning faith. So, whatever the great man says, he should add, with all the emphasis of which he is capable: 'The moment you begin to hit the ball, forget what I told you and never think of it again.'

I did not discover with certainty whether my friend desired these good offices to be tendered only by a player to his adversary or whether the system should extend to all members of the club. Personally, I should only agree with him in the first case. When a perfect stranger shall tap me on the shoulder and say: 'Excuse me, sir, but you would play much better if you did not tie yourself into such a ridiculous and complicated knot,' then, even though it be Christmas time, I shall think that the system of promiscuous benevolence has gone too far.

STANDING UP OR SITTING DOWN
(1914)

At first sight it may appear flippant and unseemly to be playing golf or talking about it at this moment. We may very well have no great inclination to do either; but it is important for everyone to keep well and fit for his work, whatever it may be, and to lead a sane and rational existence in which exercise plays a moderate part. It is a good thing, moreover, to take the mind, if possible, off gloomy and anxious matters, if even for the shortest time, and therefore one may hope not to be misunderstood if one continues to write about a game in the midst of tremendous issues.

It is possible to classify putters—the players, not the clubs—in innumerable different ways. There is, for example, the division into those two most unequal classes, the good putters and the bad putters. There is another that suggests itself to me on looking at the picture of that very excellent putter, Mr Graham Murray, namely, the division into those who stand up to the ball and those who sit down to it. Most of us, being bad putters, are thoroughly dissatisfied with our methods. Half of the world that stands up to its putts envies the other half that stoops, with its nose close to the ball, thinking that the grovelling attitude looks so comfortable and confident and gives so much control over the club. Meanwhile, the grovelling half, painfully conscious of knees bent like those of an old cab horse, and elbows sticking out in every direction, envies the upstanding brigade its grace and freedom, its martial and defiant pose; it looks at a photograph of Mr John Low and tears its hair in impotent anguish. It would be very foolish to assert that one way is necessarily right and the other necessarily wrong; but one may venture to note one or two points in regard to the question.

For one thing, it is rather interesting to observe that there are two classes of persons who stand up to their putts more than we do, and by 'we' I mean the general ruck of male British golfers. These two classes are the Americans and the ladies, and both have been frequently stated to putt much better than we do: a statement of which I am personally inclined to admit the truth as regards the Americans, and to deny, totally and ungallantly, as regards the ladies. As regards the point of style, assuming that the generalisation is correct, some reason for it may be discerned in both cases. Ladies could hardly adopt a pronouncedly grovelling or straddling stance with the club gripped but a few inches above the head. It would be lamentably unbecoming, whereas most ladies, whether they hit the ball into the hole or not, look noticeably graceful and at ease upon the putting green. American golfers stand up to the ball, not for the sake of looks, but to some extent, I suspect, because they use aluminium putters, and in particular the Schenectady. The Schenectady is essentially a club which demands that the player should grip the leather and not the shaft, and should stand fairly upright. For some reason which is rather a mysterious one, nobody has ever succeeded in putting well in a crouching manner with the club made famous by Mr Travis and Mr Travers.

Whatever may have been the exact influence exerted by

the Schenectady, the fact certainly remains that American golfers, as a race, hold their clubs near the top of the leather and stand very upright. We saw an extreme example in the styles of McDermott and Brady, two distinguished professionals who played in the Open Championship last year; both stood like soldiers on parade, bolt upright, with heels together, legs as stiff as ramrods. The feature of this style is that the player holds his body very stiff and very still, and trusts to the true swinging of the club by the wrists. On the whole, it may be said to be more generally effective than our more nondescript and happy-go-lucky methods, but it has, perhaps, this disadvantage, that it is not always a very good style in emergencies and difficulties.

This, or something like it, has been pointed out before, and by a much better critic; but it may fairly be answered that an upstanding style need not be a too mechanical and unadaptable one. Speaking as a confirmed and hopeless groveller of long experience, I honestly believe that it is far easier to contract vicious habits in sitting down to the ball than in standing up to it.

No doubt it is possible to avoid these vices and yet get well down to the putt. I may again point to the picture of Mr Graham Murray, who, with his little lofted cleek, is as deadly as need be. It will be seen that he has his nose very near the ground, and grips his club very far down the shaft, but both his legs and his arms are but little bent, and, mark the result, that he does not look in the least degree cramped; his knees and his elbows are not getting in the way. Of the many rules for putting which I have never been able to keep, I believe one of the soundest to be that the arms should hang fairly straight down from the shoulders. If we can do that, then I believe that we may grovel as much as we like. If one cannot, then we shall soon find ourselves tied into a hopeless knot and had better give up grovelling as a bad job and stand up like Grenadiers.

GOLF GOES TO WAR
(1918)

It was once believed at home that the members of the Salonica Force did nothing but sit in Mr Flocca's restaurant. Now that it is known that they did some work and had malaria, it may be stated that they sometimes amused themselves, among other things, by playing golf. The exact number of courses in Macedonia I do not know, but I played upon six and walked over two or three more besides. There was one Corps course and two Divisional courses, the others belonging as a rule to hospitals, convalescent camps and depôts; and there was at least one Battery course, where Mr Ivo Whitton, the Australian champion, taught his fellows to pitch mashie shots around the gunpits. Clubs and balls—especially balls—were precious. At one or two courses there was a slender common stock: some people had their own and expected periodic consignments of balls from home with anxiety, that deepened into gloom when there came the regular rumour that a mail boat had gone down. They could also be obtained in driblets from the EFC, and the Red Cross had a few curious weapons with springy shafts and distorted heads. One of these, to which I have no legal title, now reposes in my bag.

The course of the——Corps was on the road between Kukus and Snevce, close to the ruined and desolate village of Gramatna. It was attached to an officers' convalescent camp, but any convalescent officer who could have compassed the eighteen holes should instantly have been returned to duty. It was magnificent in conception and, if the war had only gone on another two years or so, would doubtless have been a golf course. But there were too many boulders, too thick undergrowth, and too much ploughed field. The professional, Jimmy Hunter, formerly of Richmond, toiled at it heroically, assisted by a band of Macedonian little boys with red sashes round their little stomachs; but a course of constant and mutual cheating alone made the game possible. 'I say, I'm wedged tight under a rock,' one would shout to one's partner, after a fine straight tee shot. 'How are you lying?' 'Pretty bad,' would come the answer. 'At the bottom of a rut. I think I *might* just move it, but I haven't got a niblick.' 'Well, look here, let's both tee our balls': and the game proceeded again. I once played two rounds of Gramatna in one day.

The —— Division's course of Galavanchi was, by comparison, demoralising through its easiness, for here was a fine expanse of turf with no bunkers except some old shell holes, which were too far from the greens to be of much use. They had been made when there had been troops there, but the Bulgar gunners did not interfere with legitimate amusement; and, though doubtless they saw us from the top of 535 studying our putts, scorned to interrupt the game.

There were quite presentable greens and one excellent and ubiquitous hazard, a stream of such ingenious windings that one crossed it some four times in the nine holes. Macedonia is a great country for streams and tortuous river beds, that are dry one minute and the next filled by a raging torrent. These are invaluable as hazards; and I have grateful recollections of another course, that of the Labour Depôt on the famous Ceres Road, that is entirely made by the twist-ings of a rocky stream. The course of the Infantry Base Depôt at Summerhill, not far off (how many weary, waiting soldiers have cursed the name of Summerhill!), had ravines of a truly appalling depth and rockiness, where the topper of tee shots met a well deserved fate. If one negotiated the ravine, one reached a green of bare earth set on a steep slope with a hole the size of a small jam pot. I once won a foursome there because my partner and I seldom took more than four putts on the green.

A really delightful little course was that of the forty-first Hospital at Samli, some few miles out of Salonique. It was blessed with the most lovely, delicate turf and a sandy soil, and no one could ask for faster, smoother and, I will add, more demoniacally difficult greens. There were only a very few holes that could not be reached from the tee; neverthe-less, it was the part of a modest man to reckon his score by an average of fours rather than threes. This hospital was devoted to Serbians, and there was a wonderful Serbian blacksmith who not only made a holecutter, but copied admirably any iron clubhead given to him. How he did it I do not know, but the Serb works in a mysterious way. Lavish on him a box of carpenter's tools and he will only cut his fingers, but throw him an old file and he will build you a house.

I have kept till the last the course I love best, both because I laid it out myself and because it provided the only pleasant or even bearable moments in many miserable months. It was situated on the great stretch of turf on the Monastir Road a little beyond Dudular Station, and, if we only could have obtained the labour, there is no saying what it might not have been. The turf was excellent, giving good lies everywhere, with a hardy bristle in it which withstood even the scorching Macedonian sun. We had ditches and roads and rushes and railway lines and two real bunkers—deep, sandy pits with formidable ramparts, whether connected with agriculture or relics of the last Balkan War we could never determine. Greens we had none, so we dug rather large holes with a trowel and coaxed the ball into them with mashies as best we could. We marked the holes with large stones painted white and placed on the edge of the green. They were so heavy that even a Greek would not steal them.

None of us, I suppose, will ever forget our first hole with its wonderful island green, ruined by the RAMC with their nonsensical notions of draining the surrounding swamp because mosquitos lived there. And there was the fifth hole, where the savage, wolfish dogs came and barked at us from the little farmstead; and the 'skull' hole, so called from the grisly 'flag' we marked it with, a truly noble hole perched between the railway line—that was the devil, and the road—that was the deep sea. There was the pretty 'valley' hole, where the little gipsy girl would come fawning and whining with her 'Dona penny, Johnny,' and first long hole with the handsome shepherd who piped to his sheep and found our lost balls for us at thirty leptas a ball. These things it will always be pleasant to remember—as long as we never see them again.

CONFESSIONS OF A PRACTISER
(1919)

At a certain pleasant house where I have spent year after year a winter golfing holiday there is an ancient Scottish retainer. He is now, alas! past work, but for many successive winters he used to greet me with a hardy annual joke: 'We've put you in the big room, Mr Darwin, so that you can play golf when you have a mind to it.' I had just once, after a day of peculiarly gross errors on the green, taken a putter to bed with me and practised against the legs of the chairs, and I was never afterwards allowed to forget it. It is the sort of reputation that one can never lose, and, indeed, I am afraid I have deserved it during most of my golfing life. It has probably done more harm than good, given more pain than pleasure; but the habit is almost impossible to break, and I must still confess myself an inveterate and almost unrepentant indoor practiser.

In my rooms at Cambridge I wore two holes through the carpet by means of my stance, to the great distress of my bedmaker, so that I had to get a piece of linoleum to cover up the eyesore and so propitiate her. I have putted, till my back ached, over the floor of a verandah at a small hole between two slabs of slate. I have even putted on the floor boards of a bell tent at the pole. I have played short pitches into a capacious armchair. I have tethered myself by the leg to a bedpost in order to prevent my body from swaying or my knee from bending. I have employed a strange device, blessed by Harry Vardon, whereby a string was fastened at one end to the player's cap and at the other to a piece of metal that slid up and down a groove in a post. If the player moved his head ever so slightly that confounded piece of metal began to slide up the post before his eyes; I am not sure that it did not even ring a bell. In short, if there is any folly which any reader has committed he may be sure that I, too, have committed it.

Moreover, your true practising lunatic does not confine himself to places where he can use a real club and a real ball. If he cannot swing a club he will swing the fire irons; if there is no room even for a poker, then a paper knife: nay, he will swing away vigorously without any weapon at all. A golfer of my acquaintance was one day holding forth at some length on this subject, declaring that the proper way to practise was to take out all your clubs, without any balls, and practise swinging them one after the other. 'I don't agree with you at all,' said another golfer, growing perhaps a little restive under the discourse. 'The proper way is to take out no clubs, but a box of balls, and practise keeping your eye on the ball.' His remark had the desired effect; nevertheless, I would not utterly condemn the theories that he found so tedious. Certainly I can recall many occasions when I have swung myself into what Sam Weller called an 'appleplexy' with no compensating benefits whatever, but there have also been just a few when I have hit upon the secret. One in particular was at Sandwich just before the Bar *versus* Stock Exchange match—a very good match it was incidentally, and it is a pity that it was given up. On that Friday evening I was slicing so contemptibly and continuously that ten down with eight to play seemed to stare me in the face for next day's match. I rushed desperately back to the Bell and swung away in my room—it may have been with an umbrella, or it may have been with a toothbrush—until the last available moment before dressing for dinner. When I had tried everything in vain and was beginning to think that I should have to miss the soup, a sudden inspiration sent my arms whirling freely away after the imaginary ball. I dashed down to dinner with hair unbrushed, but filled with a new and satisfying creed. Next day I drove, as you may say, like a printed book and defeated a doughty opponent by an agreeably large margin.

It must be admitted, however, that this comes near to being the exception that proves the rule, and these overnight inspirations more often than not prove sadly disillusioning in the morning. They have an extremely disturbing effect, so that you know no peace of mind until you have actually tested the new theory with club and ball. If the first two or three shots are successful a blessed calm settles down upon you: the restless craving is appeased and you are probably in for a spell of decent play—until the next breakdown; but if, which is more likely, the ball does not go as you have hoped, why then you have wearied your brain and body to no purpose and your last state is much worse than your first.

I have one particularly tragic memory of indoor practising, not my own, but somebody else's. He was a gentleman well advanced in middle life, but of a youthful and passionate keenness. We stayed together at an hotel for a meeting and as he had never before played in a team match his eagerness was almost painful. He lost his match by six holes. Nobody dared to condole, and he shut himself up in his room to swing away the memory of that black disgrace. For some time those listening without heard only the recurrent swish of the club. Then came a fearful crash and he was discovered plucking himself of bits of glass amid the ruins of a chandelier. He went to bed at eight, caught the half-past six train next morning and the meeting knew him no more.

To turn for a moment from the lighter and more ridiculous aspects of the subject, there is no doubt that many a golfer who thinks that he is practising most virtuously is really doing nothing of the sort. He takes out a caddie, half a dozen balls and a club of which he is particularly fond. The caddie goes out into the long field, the player tees his six balls in a row and slogs them merrily away and then the caddie brings them back again. This may be excellent fun or exercise, though personally I like to do my practising in secret; but it can rarely do any good. You can scarcely grow more than confident in a club, and you can waste good shots. The only practice that is really beneficial is with a club or of a stroke of which you are not the master, and in that case you must determine to take out only that recalcitrant club or to play only that particular shot. I have sometimes gone out having solemnly vowed to struggle with nothing but half-iron shots, and then yielded to the temptation to take a favourite brassie with me as well. When twilight has at last fallen, or all my balls have been lost in the heather, I have found to my extreme mortification that I have done nothing but slash gaily with the brassie, and those confounded half-iron shots have been postponed once more. Again, even if you do harden your heart and toil away at the iron shots, there is a temptation to do so in some pleasantly open spot and at no particular mark. But a half-iron shot in the abstract is of very little use. In a real game it has to be played up to a flag, and it is the fact of there being bunkers to right and left of that flag that makes your shots so crooked. If you are in a very bad way indeed the nice open space may be allowable for a stroke or two, but you must not pamper yourself too long. Sooner or later you must put it to the touch of the bunkers.

A GOLFER AND HIS SHOES
(1920)

Every golfer has a favourite pair of golfing shoes. They are comfortable and he feels at home in them, but why they suit him or what are their technical merits he very seldom knows. He gets no further than thinking that So-and-So makes them better than anyone else and will make him another pair when the present pair become too disreputable looking. I was entirely ignorant on the subject until, a few days ago, when I had the advantage of a lecture from a friend who is an acknowledged expert on the subject and also a sound and experienced golfer. He showed me models and shoes in various stages: he took pieces of brown paper and sharp weapons and cut out patterns like greased lightning; he explained the meaning of strange words to me, and I have tried to remember what he told me.

The foundation of all shoes is the model, for as the model is so will the shoe be also. Models are made of wood and resemble to the layman's eye glorified trees. For a golf shoe you want a 'short fitting,' and not an 'extended,' model. This means that the human toe must come close against the shoe's toe. Golf shoes must therefore be comparatively inelegant, since they must not come to a slender and graceful point, for that means an empty space in which no real toe is. If there is this wasted space the shoe crumples as you turn on the foot, which makes you uncomfortable and unstable and is bad for the shoe into the bargain. Next the amount of 'spring' is important. In other words, the shoe should to some extent turn up at the toe. It should not stand flat upon the ground as a smart shoe does. The flatter the model the more pronounced will be the crease across the foot as it moves in the swing, and this hurts your foot and wears the leather. The 'spring' also makes for a freer turn, but this is of secondary importance to the other points. A good deal can be done to help the foot to move in the way it should go by making the model on what my friend calls the 'rocking horse' principle. This expression is perhaps rather an alarming one; it conveys to my mind something too much of that swaying movement against which the textbooks warn us, and indeed in my own fierce and exuberant waggle I have sometimes imagined myself looking far too much like that very identical animal. But there is really no cause for alarm. I was shown one of these 'rocking horse' models and can best describe it in golfing language by saying that the sole looks like the face of a slightly 'bulged' driver. The help that it would give to the swing would be but the gentlest persuasion, scarcely more than a hint.

Then there is the question of heels. These, I am told, should be long, square 'jockey' heels like those of a riding boot. They are so called because they are made long to take the stirrup in the waist of the boot for those who ride 'home.' Their golfing merit is that they get your balance well back. A short, deep heel tends to pitch you forward on to your nose. I have seen golf shoes made with practically no heels at all and cross-examined my expert on this point. He replied that the great thing was to be natural, and he would always make a golf shoe as like a man's normal shoe as possible, except that the heel might be just a little lower and squarer. *A propos* this point I have often felt rather chary—and so, I know, do other golfers—of changing suddenly on hard summer ground from ordinary shoes to tennis shoes. One has the sensation of an altered balance from the absence of heels. This, it appears, is to some extent a matter of imagination, for a good tennis shoe is made with a 'wedge heel' which, though not perceptible from the outside, gives a 'raise' practically equal to that of the ordinary low heel, let us say about three-quarters of an inch. This, of course, does not apply to sand shoes or gymnasium shoes, which really have no more heel than they seem to have. As to what is to be put on the soles, rubber studs are suggested as giving the soundest grip either on dry, burnt ground, or on slimy clay. They are very comfortable, and are also good friends to the greenkeeper as compared with heavy nails.

Now we come to the cut of the uppers. Here the depth of the front should not be great, for the greater it is, the stiffer it is in bending. The front should be cut 'square and open,' but the 'opening' does not mean, as you or I would imagine, the place where the laces come in. It really means the curve of the 'vamp'; that is, the seam where the front joins the facing part. At the same time the model should be designed so as to clip closely at the 'quarters,' *i.e.,* what I should call the back part of the shoe, and should be low and well under the ankle bone. The leather for the uppers should be at once stout, flexible and waterproof. It is made of 'ooze calf' specially dressed. I found something my expert did not know. His views on the word 'ooze' were those of the famous cricketer as to the word 'yorker.' The great Mr Murray's dictionary does not know either, unless I have been a careless reader in that tremendous book. The only help it gives is in such quotations as 'His doeskin boots were oozing out water,' and that is the very last meaning that my shoe-making friend would like. Perhaps someone else can enlighten me. I reverently felt some of this calf and thought the name not inappropriate; it seemed to ooze through my fingers, so soft and pliable was it. The leather of which ordinary uppers are made seemed more brittle and less flexible, though it may look more beautifully polished.

Of ladies' golf shoes there are two types to suit two types of golfing ladies. For those whose golf is not too serious I was shown a pair of shoes so tiny, pointed and elegant that they might have suited Miss Knag's uncle 'who had such small feet that they were no bigger than those which are usually joined to wooden legs—the most symmetrical feet, Madame Mantalini, that even you can imagine.' But these the thorough-going player despises; hers are made on the 'short-fitting' model and are simply men's shoes in miniature.

My last piece of cross-examination was on the subject of boots as against shoes. We know that Braid and Taylor play in boots, and we have sometimes felt, when we were moving our bodies over-much and pirouetting too freely on the toes, that a pair of shooting boots would be useful in anchoring us to the ground. The oracle was in favour of shoes, though he said that he could quite understand a heavy man preferring boots if he felt that he wanted support for his ankles or his weight. The general motive for wearing shoes was, he thought, that they looked neater, more especially with knickerbockers, and certainly a pair of knickerbockered and stockinged legs terminating in large boots are not in the least beautiful.

THE OLDEST CLUB
(1920)

The Royal Blackheath Golf Club is the oldest golf club in the world. Any golfer who has in him a spark of reverence and of romance, when he first steps on to that broad expanse of heath and hits a golf ball, possibly out of rather a bad lie, must feel that he is on hallowed ground. And it is one of the delightful things about going to Blackheath that those who play there have palpably so sturdy a pride in their ancient society and so romantic an affection for everything that belongs to it. When Mr Robert Whyte, now holding that unique position among golf clubs of Field-Marshal, first put on his medal of office, when Mr Lincoln, the present Captain, hung the silver ball, emblem of his captaincy, to the silver club, they felt, I know very well, that it was theirs to carry on a great tradition of friendliness and hospitality and golf as it should be played, and to that tradition the whole club lives up.

There is a sad gap in the history of Blackheath. Like some other clubs, it had a disastrous fire at the end of the eighteenth century. Tradition says that James I, when he came from Scotland, played there with his courtiers, and that a society of golfers was formed under Royal patronage in 1608; but it is not till 1787 that there is written proof of its existence. From that date onwards minutes and betting books tell us something of its history. That history has been collected together with loving pains in Mr W. E. Hughes's *Chronicles of Blackheath Golfers*, and Mr Hughes has allowed me to quote whatever I like from his engaging book. Without his kind help I should not dare to write about the club, and, even as it is, I do so with great diffidence.

There is much historical lore to touch upon. Yet I must not let any reader think that Blackheath lives only in the past. To play on the heath is not merely to experience the charm of what is old. It is to play a game exciting in itself, full of interesting chances and hazards, giving scope for boldness and originality and making you realise your own limitations as a golfer. It is anything but cut-and-dried golf. There is the green perched up on a little plateau perhaps just beyond a grass-grown gravel pit or nestling on a little triangle of turf guarded by intersecting roads, and you must exercise your ingenuity as to the best way to get there. You may see two red-coated golfers far apart, not because one or both of them have driven erratically, but because each has his own notion of the best way of reaching that hole; nor is it possible to say that either of them is wrong.

You must sometimes cast away preconceived ideas, such as that, if there is a cross hazard guarding a green, it is your bounden duty to pitch over it. When the ground is hard you may have to pitch your ball short of that road in such a way that it will leap across to stay on the green. If it does not leap aright you may be playing a niblick shot from under a hard perpendicular ledge. That is the chance you must take and make the best of it, and very good discipline, too, now and again, for you, oh-too-modern golfer. Nor is only ingenuity called for. Blackheath, as is well known, has among its seven holes two of the longest in the world following one another. They do not seem so long now as they did when Mr 'Freddy' Ireland used to bang his gutty ball along with a driving mashie and devilish skill from those flinty hard lies. They must be short indeed compared with what they were in the days when, on March 18, 1797, it was solemnly recorded that 'Mr Longlands this day holed the Ball at the long Hole in six strokes and the wind NE, stiff breeze.'

Mr Longlands, I suspect, had five fine full drives with his feathery ball and then holed a great putt at the end of them. But those holes still call for strong hitting by a man who can deal faithfully with the ball where it lies, often on a patch of bare and stony ground. It is a curious and strenuous game that you play at Blackheath. Perhaps it is not one to play too often: but it demands sterling qualities. If ever you feel inclined to look down on it, just ask yourself this question: 'Is this the course on which you would choose to play someone you are afraid of, someone who is better than you?' The answer would always, I think, be in the negative, and that is some testimony of the qualities of the course. 'Rough he may be,' said Mr Elijah Pogram. 'So air our Barrs. Wild he may be. So air our Buffalers. But he is a child of Natur' and a child of Freedom.' The Blackheath golfer might utter something of the same defiance on his course's behalf. You may not like it, but you can hardly afford to despise it.

And now we must get to our history. That word in connection with Blackheath will at once bring one thing into the mind of the average golfer, namely, Lemuel Abbott's delightful picture of Mr William Innes in his uniform of red coat and blue facings and a single epaulet as a past Captain of the club. His caddie, with the bottle protruding from his pocket, is a 'College man,' a pensioner of the Royal Naval Hospital at Greenwich, and the background shows us Morden College, Shooter's Hill and Severn Droog Castle. There is an excellent print in the club, but the actual picture, alas! is not there, and Mr Hughes tells me that he has never been able to find any evidence that it now exists. It was painted in 1790, and it is possible that it was destroyed in the fire a few years afterwards, but nothing is known of it. Ninety years after that picture was painted Mr Francis Bennoch was Captain of the club, and he had the quaint thought of having himself painted in the Innes manner, though in more modern costume. In the background is seen the Ranger's House in Greenwich Park. These two names of Innes and Bennoch, separated by so long an interval, are both Scottish, and the Society of Golfers at Blackheath was, until golf became a universal game, a society of Scotsmen, who played their native game though in exile. This is apparent when we read the list of Captains or medal winners. Practically all are Scotsmen until in 1812 we come suddenly upon one Gotlieb Christian Ruperti. Who he was or whence he came I know not, but he was clearly a convivial and hospitable soul worthy of the best traditions.

Both in 1812 and 1813 he presented the club with excellent haunches of venison. In 1812 during his captaincy His Serene Highness the Duke of Brunswick and the Duc de Bouillon dined at the anniversary dinner of the club, and in 1813 he was apparently the prime mover in a still greater anniversary festival. A public breakfast was given 'to the ladies and gentlemen of the Heath and its neighbourhood.' There were tents, bearing the golf flag, a regimental band and a party of soldiers to keep the ground, and the ladies, so say the minutes, 'were invited to partake of a cold collation.' After this 'the Gentlemen soon joined the ladies and the scene then became truly interesting from so large an assemblage of ladies of beauty and fashion. Swift-footed Time too soon beckoned it is the hour to part, and after the Band played God save the King the ladies took their leave with regret, but with countenances that bespoke a lively remembrance of the happy hours they had spent.' Later there was a dinner, toasts and songs, His Serene Highness of Brunswick again and another haunch of venison, 'out of the Duke of Rutland's park,' from the jovial Mr Ruperti.

Another great man in the club at the beginning of last century was Mr Henry Callender, whose fine portrait, also by Lemuel Abbott, now hangs in the hall—a splendid and dignified figure in red coat and white knee breeches. Mr Callender was Secretary in 1789 and Captain of the club in 1801 and 1807. His name appears constantly in the minutes over a long period of years. In 1800, for instance, 'Mr Callender having taken the keys of the Golf Box to Ramah Droog Castle, Captain Longlands desires notice to be taken of the same, and as "wine does wonders" a Gallon of course follows.' He was evidently very popular, for on June 11, 1807, 'Mr Walker assisted by Mr Laurie took the opportunity of expressing the regard and affection of the Club to the Chairman by placing upon his shoulder an additional Epaulet, and his health under the appellation of "Captain General" was drunk with great applause.' Less than a year afterwards the members appeared in mourning for three successive Saturdays in his memory, together with that of two other 'worthy and lamented friends.'

The deeds of these jovial old gentlemen have taken me ahead too fast. We must go back first to 1766 and then to 1787. The former date is inscribed on the silver club on which each succeeding Captain hung a silver ball until 1865, when a new one had to be provided for succeeding Captains. The old club is inscribed 'August 16, 1766, the gift of Mr Henry Foot to the Honourable Company of Goffers at Blackheath.' In 1787 comes the first piece of writing, a list of subscribers to the club who met at the Chocolate House, Blackheath. This was the club's first meeting place. Subsequently the assembly rooms were moved to the Green Man and the golfers went there for their dinner. This dinner was clearly an important part of the proceedings. The club season lasted from April to the beginning of November, and on every Saturday during that time the club met to play. After the play came the dinner, and at dinner bets were made and recorded in a bet book which comes down to us from 1791.

Sometimes they were on subjects of general interest, such as this on September 1, 1792: 'Mr Duff lays Mr Turner a Hogshead of Claret that Monsieur Dumourier, now Commander of the Northern Army of France, was not advanced to the rank of Colonel in the French service previous to the present Revolution. Mr Turner lays the contrary. Lost and paid honourably by Mr Duff. T. Longlands, Chair.' More often they were on golf matches. In April, 1792, 'Mr Longlands bets Mr Wm. Innes, senior, that he will play him for a gallon of claret, giving Mr Innes one stroke in each hole. Four rounds on the green, out and in holes to be played,' and there is added this, which we may almost call the first recorded allusion to the nineteenth hole: 'It is understood that if they come in equal. One hole additional is to be played to determine this Bet.' Once a year there was a more gorgeous dinner on the anniversary day of the club, and it was on this day that the princely Ruperti presided over that splendid festival graced by the ladies and the regimental band.

There were many keen golfers who did not like to go without their golf or their jolly dinners during the off season in the winter, and it was chiefly, no doubt, on this account that the rather mysterious Knuckle Club was founded. Such minutes as exist show that the club met every Saturday at certain times of the year to have dinner, including 'a dish of soup and knuckles, particularly beef ones.' They also seem to have had some element of freemasonry. There was a sign, a process of initiation, and answers to questions to be learnt. The rules, too, laid down a certain ceremonial, such as that 'No member shall speak on matters relating to the club longer than five minutes, during which he is to hold the Knuckle in his right hand.' The members made bets and played for a gold medal, which in 1792 was won by Mr Longlands, the hero who once did the long hole in six in a wind. In 1794 our other betting friend, Mr Duff, appears. His health was drunk on the occasion of his marriage, whereupon 'that gentleman, after making a genteel speech on the occasion, presented the Club with a gallon of Claret.'

In 1825 the Knuckle Club turned into the Blackheath Winter Golf Club. The old mysteries, whatever they were, died with it and its ornaments and insignia were done away with. There is nothing very remarkable about the Winter Golf Club. It went on in the old cheerful way, discussing 'a very nice turtle' when somebody would give it one, and closing its season with 'Happy to meet, sorry to part and happy to meet again.'

There is one bet that may be quoted. It arose as to the age of Mr John Cam Hobhouse, MP for the City of Westminster, and the Registrar with solemn politeness wrote and asked Mr Hobhouse to settle the matter. The answer is a pleasant one: 'Sir, in reply to your note I have to inform you that on the 27th of next June, I shall no longer be liable to serve in the Militia. This is the only advantage I shall derive from having been born so very long ago. Your enquiry needs no apology and I am Very much your servant John C. Hobhouse.' That was in 1831. Thirteen years later, for no particular reason that Mr Hughes can tell us, the club was dissolved, and the old medal, inherited from the Knuckle, presented to the Blackheath Golf Club, so that from 1844 there is the history of but a single club.

It was in 1843 that the number of holes was increased to seven, as it still remains. Before that there were only five. This, Mr Hughes points out, was the number played by the Honourable Company of Edinburgh Golfers on Leith Links, and some Scottish exiles revived the memory of the links they had left by using two Leith names for two points on Blackheath, the Thorntree and Braehead. There were holes called the 'Assembly Rooms' hole and 'Shooters Hill' hole, which can, I believe, be roughly located, but the only quite definite fact that Mr Hughes ventures on is that the gravel pits were in old days avoided. Doubtless they were more formidable hazards then than they are today, and moreover there were plenty without them. True, there were far fewer roads, pedestrians, lamp posts and small boys' schools playing football, features of Backheath golf today; but there must have been plenty of whins.

Even now if we wander on to the corner of the heath past the long fifth hole we find an attractive bit of wild country where the whins grow thickly, and think, if it were not sacrilegious, that we might add to the course an admirable short hole or two in those dells among the bushes. In quite modern times one fine hazard, Marr's Ravine, has disappeared from the present fourth hole – filled up, more is the pity—though whether that formed part of the ancient course I do not know. Altogether we may imagine that the Blackheath golfers of old had plenty of difficulties to account for the scores that now seem rather high.

The old clubs of the early nineteenth century that are kept in the clubhouse under a glass case do not look easy to play with. To our thinking the irons are very upright and stumpy-headed. No one knows who used the tremendous iron in the middle, but he must have been a great or an eccentric man. Even the wonderful long driver that Mr Horace Hutchinson used to play with would seem simple to wield by comparison. A recorded bet gives a clue as to how far these clubs would hit a feather ball. In 1813 Mr Laing, who was subsequently a medal winner, betted that given ten chances he would drive a ball 500 feet. The scores that were done may be gathered from the lists of medal winners. In the days of the five-hole course, play was over three rounds or fifteen holes, and the two best scores appearing in those days were 105 and 104 by Mr William Black in 1822 and 1823, 104 by Mr Masson, who presented the club with its silver quaich, and in 1838 102 by Mr C. G. Anderson. In 1843, when three rounds of seven holes were first played, there was some very hard work done, and the Hon. Fox Maule won the Spring Medal with 175, but I think the honourable gentleman must have been a lucky winner or the new holes very rough, for when the Summer Medal was played under the new conditions Mr Andrew Jopp returned 129. After this the scores did not materially improve for a long time. The great Mr George Glennie did 121 in 1859, but won subsequently with 131, and the first man to break 120 was the late Dr Laidlaw Purves in 1884 with 118. Even in the Nineties 123 won the Summer Medal, and Mr F. S. Ireland's 101 in 1895, of course with a gutty, was really a great achievement. The official record with the rubber-cored ball for the seven holes is 30.

The name of George Glennie is, of course, a great one in golfing history, and it is one never to be forgotten in Blackheath history. He was elected Honorary Secretary and Treasurer in 1868 and was still working devotedly for the club at his death in 1886. The well-known George Glennie Medal at St Andrews was given by the club to the Royal and Ancient in his memory. It was Mr Glennie, too, who, from a purely playing point of view, raised Blackheath to the greatest eminence it ever attained. In 1857 the Prestwick Club proposed a tournament to be played by foursomes between eight clubs St Andrews, Perth, Musselburgh, Blackheath, Prestwick, Carnoustie, North Berwick and Leven. The tournament was played at St Andrews, and the Blackheath couple were Mr Glennie and Mr John Campbell Stewart of the 72nd Highlanders. This Mr Stewart must have been a fine golfer, for Mr Everard tells us of him that he would play level against the great Alan Robertson, and that, despising a tee, he would throw the ball down on the ground and play it as it lay. The two Blackheath champions mowed down their opponents in great style, beating the Royal and Ancient in the final and winning a most engaging silver claret jug. In the minutes of the following Spring Medal Day appears this justly proud entry: 'That Mr Glennie and Capt Stewart be elected Life Members in consideration of their having gained for the Club the prize played for at the Great Golf Tournament at St Andrews July 1857, thereby constituting this club the Champion Golf Club of the World.'

It is well known how much the Blackheath Club did to encourage the spread of golf in England when it first began to spread. There were many Blackheath golfers at Westward Ho! in the early days, likewise at Hoylake, and no longer than twenty years ago the team that used to play for Yarmouth against Cambridge was almost identical with that which treated us so hospitably and beat us so roundly on the heath. Mr Robert Whyte, now Field-Marshal of the club, the Messrs Ireland, Mr Hughes, Mr 'Jack' Gibson, the late Mr Walter Richardson, Mr Sawyer the Treasurer—these are all friendly and familiar names to generations of Cambridge golfers.

It may not be so well known that Blackheath helped on the game in earlier times and remoter regions. In 1830 it is recorded that the club read of the formation of a club at Dum-Dum, a name familiar to those who know their *Vanity Fair*,' from Jos Sedley's famous story about Miss Sophy Cutler. 'Prosperity to it,' was given from the chair with all the honours and a copy of the Blackheath rules sent to the new club. A little later, in 1842, a polite letter was despatched to the Bombay Club saying that Blackheath had heard with 'heartfelt satisfaction' of the foundation of the Bombay Golf Club and sending congratulations, a copy of the club's rules and a song composed by the Blackheath poet laureate, Mr W. Jordan, 'upon the occasion of his first seeing the game of golf played.'

In due course there arrived an equally polite answer from the Bombay secretary, Mr Buist. This gentleman, who joked with some difficulty, was very facetious about an imaginary golfing deputation from Blackheath. They were to find '54 miles of excellent play ground' in the desert between Cairo and Suez and there were allusions to a 'celebrated putting ground and holes at Corinth and excellent hazards at Thermopylae.' In the following year the Bombay Club sent a medal, which was lost on the wreck of the *Memnon*. A second medal was more fortunate and is now among the treasured medals of the Blackheath club, who, in 1856, returned the attention by voting a gold medal to Bombay. A good deal later, in 1875, there was an exchange of compliments with the Calcutta Club, who sent the beautiful silver cup, made in Cashmere, which is still played for.

With this Calcutta Cup we come to comparatively modern golfing times from the point of view of so ancient a club and I shall not trace its history down to the present except to mention various changes of clubhouse. In 1843 a house was taken in College Place, Royal Hill. Six years later a move was made to near the top of Blackheath Hill. In 1865 a house was taken a little lower down the hill and finally only a few years ago there was a last move to the present club, Heath Hill House, a pleasant countryfied house, standing in a little garden, surrounded by a wall and looking straight out on the green stretch of heath. Close under the wall is the last putting green, a beautifully natural undulating little green, a fine site for the ending of a match.

This house is full of interesting pictures of all kinds, portraits of Field-Marshals and Captains, groups of members, sketches, caricatures and photographs, a wonderful collection, to which I cannot do full justice here. One, and a very pleasant one, is that of Alick Brotherston, 'Old Alick,' who was a caddie and afterwards 'hole maker' to the club. He was born in 1756, went to sea from Leith in 1769, and died in 1840. On the back of his picture is a sheet of paper on which the old sailor wrote down in his own strictly phonetic spelling the names of the various ships in which he had sailed. Thus the *Asia* appears as 'Ashey,' the *Leda* as 'Ledy,' and Captain Campbell who commanded the *Dragan* is 'Camell.' The picture is by Mr Gallen 'of Greenwich School.' Another striking portrait is that of Mr George Lindsay, who was Field-Marshal of the club from 1831 to 1857. It is by Francis Grant, RA, afterwards Sir Francis Grant, PRA, who was captain of the club and presented the portrait to it.

And here I must take leave of this famous and venerable society of golfers with many thanks to the committee of the club for their kindness in unlocking their many treasures. 'Prosperity to it,' as the golfers of Blackheath drank to those of Dum-Dum. *Floreat florebit.*

MIXED FOURSOMES
(1921)

I have just been engaged in an affair at once daring and delicate. I have screwed up my courage to make a proposal to a lady—to be my partner in a mixed foursome tournament. I am glad to say that she did not keep me in suspense 'according,' as Mr Collins said in *Pride and Prejudice*, 'to the usual practice of elegant females,' and I now have an admirable partner to pull me along in what should be a most entertaining competition. This tournament is to take place at Worplesdon on October 24, 25 and 26, and ought to be delightfully novel and interesting. Really good mixed doubles at golf are rare. We have seen the best ladies engaged in pitched battles against good men, but, on the whole, it is better fun to watch them playing against each other, because in the Stoke Poges fights they have sometimes seemed rather crushed by mere brute force. In a mixed foursome they will not suffer in that respect, and their extreme accuracy ought to make them most valuable allies. I shall be surprised if some of the couples do not play rounds very nearly, if not quite, as good as the arrogant male partner could play all by himself.

Let us now pass from the rarified atmosphere of tournaments to the ordinary average mixed foursome, such as may be seen at the present moment on many seaside courses. It is a delightful amusement for those who play in it; not quite so delightful sometimes for those who play behind it. It would generally, I think, be better fun for all parties if it were played on the terms that the ladies drove from their own tees. I have occasionally fancied, when following in the wake of such a foursome on a 'holiday' course, that it would be better if the gentlemen also adopted this modest policy; but that is another story. If the ladies decide heroically to drive from the men's tees they are sometimes confronted with carries such that their best shots must be bunkered, and that is no fun for anybody. If they drive from their own, then it should be an admirable game and one that always seems to me a fine test of the male golfer's skill and nerve. He must do everything he reasonably can to gain length, or else at the end of two shots there will be just a little bit of distance left over and the alliance will not reach the green in the orthodox number of strokes. At the same time he must not take big risks in the way of big bunkers because, once in a bunker, it is 'the usual practice of elegant females' to stay there. The really good lady player is very good out of bunkers; there is, for instance, no greater artist in sand than Miss Grant Suttie, and Miss Leitch is likewise magnificent out of any abominably bad place. But there is, in this respect, a great gulf fixed between the very good and the ordinary; the average lady player never seems quite to have grasped the principle that the way to get out of a bunker is to clench the teeth and hit venomously and blasphemously hard; or perhaps it is that she has not the strength to act on it. At any rate, it is much the best policy not to give her the chance of doing so, and she has every right to complain of a partner who does not obey the cardinal rule of foursome golf and 'keep the ball in play.'

Again, the man has always to look ahead and consider

whether he is leaving the lady to make too dangerous and desperate a frontal attack upon the green. Many a man is comparatively brave when he has a bunker in front of him and will make a good enough shot; what frightens him and makes him go crooked is a narrow way between flanking hazards. With the average lady player it is, I think, rather the other way. She is courageous and trustworthy when it is a question of steering between Scylla and Charybdis; but when there is a chasm between her and the flags her partner must await the result with nervously averted eyes. Because she is not, as a rule, very strong in the hands and wrists, she is not very good at getting the ball into the air, and moderately bad lie makes it proportionately much more difficult for her. The man must therefore do some manœuvring for position and remember that in a mixed foursome the longest way round is often the shortest way home.

The lady's nerve, too, is tested, and that in a particularly trying way. She knows, or she ought to know (her partner, if he is a reasonably gallant man, cannot tell her so) that whether she hits a little longer or shorter, whether she takes her brassie through the green or her driving iron, does not so very greatly matter. What is required of her is a high standard of blamelessness in small things—and steady putting. Now, we all know that the shot wherein nothing is wanted but that we should keep out of trouble, is just the one with which we go most crooked; also that when we particularly want to putt well we putt most ill. That being so, the poor lady's lot is not so very easy or happy a one. Of course, as I said before, all these rather unchivalrous remarks apply only to the common or garden foursome. At Worplesdon all I shall try to do is to hit the mildest little 'shotties' down the course and my partner will do all the rest.

THE DISSEMBLING GOLFER
(1922)

I have lately been reading Mr Sidney Fry's book on billiards, with very great interest if with no hope of improving my own game, which is, indeed, played but once a year and is wholly a matter of chance. In his chapter of reminiscences there is a story of how, by way of a small joke, he was once introduced to a fellow guest as Mr 'Roast' instead of Mr Fry, and under that title played him two matches, one at billiards and the other at golf. At billiards he managed to dissemble and make a close match of it by playing left-handed, with occasional, and for the most part undetected, recourse to his right hand in case of emergency. At golf he masqueraded as a twelve handicap player, his opponent being fourteen, and here he was a less polished actor or else his energy gave out, for he won too easily, by 6 and 5.

The story set me thinking how very difficult it is to dissemble at golf. It is not, of course, a thing to be done seriously; but most of us have tried to do it at one time or another, either in a 'rag' game or out of some momentary feeling of pity towards a completely crushed opponent, and we have generally made but a poor job of it. I have once seen it extraordinarily well done by somebody else in a foursome that was intended by two of the parties to come, by hook or by crook, to the last hole. My friend, whom I will call G., a very fine golfer, and I were the two tigers of the party: the two rabbits play golf only once a year. They both played for all they were worth, and for a while the match was closely fought. But my poor rabbit, who was not very well, fell away: he missed the ball twice at one hole, both times with his putter, and we became several holes down. Then G. rose to wonderful heights. Playing the one off three he drove the ball into inaccessible spots, with a most life-like show of vexation. Once he was stymied, but the balls were but three inches apart, and a tactless caddie pointed out that the obstructing ball might be removed. 'Ah, my boy,' said G., 'you aren't up to date. The rule has been changed'; and he forthwith knocked our ball into the hole in the most natural way in the world. Even so we were still one down with two to play: G. had a short putt on the seventeenth green to win the match, and our ball was on the other side of the hole. I waited breathlessly to see how his genius would find a way out. He did it by playing as brilliant a shot as ever I saw, just missing the hole, just touching our ball and cannoning off it at just such an angle as to leave his own rabbit a dead and hopeless stymie. And so the match was halved, and I really do not think that our two rabbits had any serious suspicions until the very end.

On a subsequent occasion I had to attempt something of the same sort myself, and then I realised to the full what a great man G. was. True, I missed a putt or two—anybody can do that—but it would not have availed if my fellow-tiger had not holed some very good ones, and that is a thing that very few people can do exactly when they want. As to my efforts in the long game, they were a miserable failure. I remember at one short-hole tee walking up to the ball with a fine assumption of reckless, devil-me-care swagger such as I hoped would produce a devastating top, and behold! the ball soared away beautifully, had a lucky kick into the bargain, and finished dead at the hole side. No, it is not an easy business to carry through with any artistic verisimilitude. The next time I essay it, I must remember the advice of one of the canniest and most cunning golfers of my acquaintance. This is, never to leave it to the green, where the fierce light of your opponent's eye beats right upon you, nor in any case to try deliberately to miss a shot, because you will probably hit it by mistake. The game is, he declares, to take the wrong club through the green. Then you may play a perfectly respectable shot that will escape notice. If you under-club yourself, the ball, though well enough struck, will quite naturally fall into the bunker short of the green: if you over-club, it will plunge into the deep heather beyond it. Your judgment may be impugned, but not your *bona fides*.

There is, if I remember rightly, in one of Harry Vardon's books a story of how, on his first visit to America, he and some brother professionals visited on an off-day a little rustic course. For several holes they amused themselves by pretending to be beginners and asking their caddies to instruct them: then, growing weary of missing the ball, they began to play their natural game. The caddies, feeling themselves insulted, thereupon threw down their clubs and marched off the course in a body. I recollect also to have heard a somewhat similar story, possibly apocryphal, of one of the visits of Vardon and Ray to America. They went to a small course, where they were not known by sight, and took out the local professional. He, however, had the laugh on his side, for when they revealed their identity he remained wholly unimpressed, declared that he had never heard the names of either Ray or Vardon and stuck to it stoutly to the end.

At any rate, I believe it is quite true that, in the summer of 1921, a very good American amateur, Mr 'Reggie' Lewis, was dressed up to personate a distinguished British lady golfer then in the country. He played several holes, quite unsuspected, and much admired alike for his personal charms and his golf, before he suddenly cast off his disguise, to the consternation of the gallery. That, however, is a height of dissembling to which few of us can aspire.

THE PAMPERED GOLFER
(1923)

This article is not, as might perhaps be imagined from its title, an outcry against the luxury of the age and a plea for a luncheon of sandwiches and carrying one's own clubs. It is directed rather against those golfers who want the game made too easy for themselves by the elimination of all chances of what they deem undeserved disaster.

I have lately been playing on a course towards which I feel a devotion of many years, and I was pained to find in force at one hole there a local rule which seems to me an infamous one. At this hole there stretches across the course at a distance of something over 200 yards from the tee a deep and watery ditch. It cannot be carried unless by someone with the driving powers of Abe Mitchell, but when the ground is hard and there is a strong following wind the well-hit ball of an ordinary mortal may possibly reach it. The green can comfortably be attained in the second shot from a position short of the ditch, and one would imagine therefore that there was no great hardship in taking, on rare occasions, a spoon from the tee. The local pundits, however, have thought otherwise. They have staked off a portion of the ditch, which lies in the direct line to the hole, and have enacted that if the player drives into the ditch from the tee at any point between these two white posts he can lift without penalty. On the other hand, if he goes in with his second or any subsequent shot, he can only lift under penalty of a stroke.

On mature consideration I take this to be the worst local rule in the world. It is complicated, it is artificial, and it shows an entire misconception of the game of golf, which should be, in Mr John Low's words, 'a contest of risks.' To make such a rule as this is in effect to lay down this principle, that the man who, without using his intelligence, hits the ball down the middle of the course off the middle of his club is in no circumstances whatever to suffer any inconvenience. And a very poor principle it is. I quite admit that, if I do happen to hit a straight and reasonably long drive and then get into trouble, I may complain bitterly at the moment of my bad luck. It is a human weakness to do so. I also admit that constantly to be compelled to play short from the tee would make a dull game of it. But, after all, to hit a good, straight drive is not a very wonderful achievement—one ought to do it quite often—and just once in a while to have to use one's head and restrain one's energies is not a very great hardship. It is surely a hundred times preferable to this artificial and pampering rule which makes it a case of 'Heads I win and tails I can't lose.' A distinguished professional once said to me that he liked St Andrews better than any other course because (only he expressed it rather more strongly) 'you might play a very good shot there and get into a very bad place.' That is surely a more manful point of view than that which is indicated by those two wretched little white posts.

I had only just ceased from fulminating against the two posts when, oddly enough, I heard from a golfer of my acquaintance, expressing much the same views *à propos* of another and more famous course. There, so he told me, the authorities had had put before them by a scratch player a

long and solemn proposal for a number of alterations to be
made to the fairway at various holes. The object of them was
that, whatever the wind, a flat lie and a good stance should
invariably reward a good drive and that the scratch player
should thus be able to reach the green with his second,
whereas he might not be able to do it from an uphill lie. The
answer given was, I believe, something to this effect: that if
the proposed alterations were made it would be only fair to
make others to suit those with longer handicaps and shorter
driving powers, and that it would be altogether too colossal a
task to flatten out the course from 120 yards to 300 yards
from the tee. It was not added, but it might well have been,
that to do so would be entirely to ruin one of the most
charming golf courses in the world.

There is one point in the answer given to that scratch
player which is particularly worthy of notice, namely that if
hummocks are to be flattened to suit the long driver they
must also be flattened for the short. Those of us who are still
capable of hitting the ball a reasonable distance have, I
think, a very imperfect sympathy with shorter drivers. Yet
we have in point of hummocks a very easy time of it.

I realised this fully only when playing at St Andrews with
one who, having been in his day a great golfer, is now
something too stiff to hit the ball far from the tee. Time and
again his ball finished in a most difficult lie among humps
and hollows while mine—through no merit of mine, but
through the advantage of some twenty years—lay clear on
even ground. He bore it like a Trojan, but he often lost
nearly a whole stroke from the tee, and I have seen much the
same thing happen at Sandwich and at other places. It
is right that the longer of two players should have an
advantage, but one does not like to see it made more
overwhelming than need be.

We are all of us too apt to desire a course to suit our own game. I am disposed to think that my own tee shot, when I hit it, should be regarded as a standard of what is decently respectable, and that the smooth country and the bunkers should be placed accordingly. If people are so old and puny that they cannot hit so far as I do, or so young and strong that they can hit as far as Mr Tolley or Mr Wethered—well, they must take their chance. Only the other day, on a certain course, I came to what used to be a bunker and was now converted into a grassy hollow. I enquired the reason of the change. 'Oh,' was the rather bitter answer, 'I suppose So-and-so (a prominent member of the Green Committee) drove into it one day. He always has bunkers filled up when he gets into them.'

Clearly we all have to think a little more about other people's shots and a little less about our own if our opinions as to the courses on which we play are to be worth listening to. And we shall do this best by bearing in mind the principle which is so gravely transgressed by those two miserable white posts of mine. The whole game of golf does not consist in hitting the ball straight in the direction of the hole without any regard to the lie of the land, and a shot so hit is not necessarily a good shot.

Moreover, nobody, whatever the shot he has played, has an absolute and indefeasible right to a perfect lie and a perfect stance. 'I quite appreciate,' says my correspondent, 'that it would be hard for a professional to lose the Championship from having a worse lie at the -th hole (a hole of many hummocks) from no fault of his own, but I have not heard complaints from pros., only from amateurs.' If that be so, then the more shame to us amateurs who play the game for fun and have nothing to lose, save our tempers, through a bad lie or a bad stance. But I hope that we are not—most of us—quite so foolish as he thinks. Of course, we grouse at the moment, but we do not as a rule write to the Committee about it and we do not really like white posts.

HOLIDAY'S END
(1924)

A delightful artist, who amuses us with his pictures for six
days of every week in every year, gave us last week a pathetic
series representing the end of the holidays. A small boy was
shown doing everything for the very last time, from the last
bathe to the last cinema, and in each picture his eyes grew
rounder and sadder, his tears larger. I do not remember that
there was a picture of him playing his last round of golf, but
at this moment many little boys and many grown-ups, too,
are engaging in that tragic ritual, and it occurred to me, who
have often written articles of gloating anticipation on the
beginning of a golfing holiday, to shed a valedictory tear over
its ending.

Fortunately, it is not quite so sad as it sounds. There is
generally a measure of compensation. I remember very well
a summer holiday of my own, when I was about nine years
old, that ended in a perfect blaze of glory. At the ninth hole
at Felixstowe there was a carry over a road and a bunker
beyond it. I suppose it may have been seventy or eighty
yards, but the exact distance is trapped in a rosy haze. At any
rate, I had never carried it: my best tee shots always went
plump into the bunker. And now with my very last drive of
the last round of the last day I sent the ball soaring over it
with several feet to spare. It was the supreme moment of a

golfing lifetime, never to be repeated, and as the train steamed away next morning I could say *Nunc dimittis* with a single heart. It never can happen again, and grown-up golfers must look elsewhere for less ecstatic sources of consolation. One of them can often be found in the subtle and devastating disease known as staleness. It is only those with wonderful strength or wonderful self-control who have not overplayed themselves by the end of a holiday. For the last few days we have felt rather jaded and creaking. We have found it harder and harder to fling ourselves at the ball with real zest, and have had to pretend that we are taking it easy, and not pressing, from a deliberate wisdom. We may have been hitting the ball with some mechanical accuracy just because our eye is in, but the careless rapture of slashing has departed, and in our hearts we know that we want a rest. And so we can pack not ungratefully under the fond delusion that a few days of repose in an office will bring back the lost sting without impairing the accuracy.

Another source of consolation may be found in the fact that our individual golfing histories have a habit of repeating themselves. We grow a little weary of making the same kind of bad shot at the same hole on the same course for round after round. M. Coué has remarked that if we think about a particular bunker we go into it, and it is painfully true. I have myself been playing more or less every day for a fortnight on the most engaging course at Aldeburgh. Every day the wind has been blowing in the same direction. It would be an exaggeration to say that I know exactly what I am going to do with every shot, but I have at least a very strong suspicion. There is, for example, that fascinating little fourth hole with its green in the form of a lop-sided island, not unlike the thirteenth at Worplesdon. On the left-hand side of the green is a kindly mountain which prevents the ball from running too far and turns it in towards the hole. Every time I say to myself on the tee, as I take my mashie-niblick in hand, 'Now, you fool, mind you play to the left.' And every time I play in fact straight on the pin. Every time my opponent says, 'That's a good one,' and every time I reply in a weary voice, 'No, it isn't; it's too strong and will run over into the bunker.' And every time that is exactly what it does.

When, on the other hand, I come to the next short hole, the eighth, precisely the opposite thing happens. I beg and pray myself to play straight at the hole, which is a perfectly simple thing to do, and in fact I go persistently and as straight as a homing pigeon for a monticle on the left. I invariably hook from the twelfth tee and I slice from the sixteenth. But stay—let me do myself justice. I *did* slice at the sixteenth into a particular gorse bush, but now for the last three rounds in succession I have hit a straight one right down the middle of the course. That is another good reason for stopping in time, lest I should begin to slice once more.

Then there is the most consoling fact of all, that we have all of us during this holiday discovered something or another which will make us play rather better for the rest of our lives. True, we seem dimly to remember having discovered something last year and the year before, and both those somethings have now been cast aside into that dusty corner where moulder our discarded theories. But, of course, we never did really quite believe in them. The fact was, in those other years we played well because we were in practice, and it amused us to pretend that we had made a discovery. This year it is, it must be, the real thing at last, for which we have waited so patiently and hopefully. All others were spurious, this is the real revelation. For myself I have done a far, far better thing than make a discovery for myself, because I have made a discovery on behalf of somebody else. I have inoculated a friend with the germ of Mr Beldam's theory of the flail, about which I wrote a few weeks ago.

I did it with the fire-irons one evening after dinner. The next day he went away to another course and actually tied with two others for the second prize in a mixed foursome competition. He and his partner received only a beggarly stroke a hole from bogey, and they finished all square. His share of the sweepstake was seven and six (37½p), and he assured me, with tears in his eyes, that he was my debtor for life. He had never before dreamed of such driving. The day following we played a single, and through some mischance I won at the twelfth hole by that same figure of seven and six. But let not the ribald disbelievers scoff! He returned to the assault, still 'flailing' gallantly and, metaphorically, knocked my head off, and he still regards me and Mr Beldam as his joint benefactors. It is true that what he gained on the swings he lost on the roundabouts because, while his driving improved, his iron play temporarily ceased to exist. However, a little solitary practice is going to put that right in less than no time. Meanwhile, as I sit writing on a balcony and looking at the sea, he is stewing in his office. But nobody need pity him. His holiday is over, but he knows that he is never going to drive badly any more. I am simply glowing with unselfish happiness. I feel as virtuous as any Boy Scout who has done his one good deed a day. I have helped a 'forlorn, forsaken brother'—or at least he thinks I have, which is the next best thing.

GOLF IN A GARAGE
(1925)

Golf is generally held to be a mild and gentle, almost a senile form of exercise. That is only because we do not as a rule hit a sufficiently large number of balls in a sufficiently short space of time. Intensive golf can be very hard exercise indeed, as anybody would have agreed who enjoyed my experience of last week.

I was bidden to lunch by a kind friend, a very busy man who lives in the heart of London. When lunch was finished we repaired to his garage, which is also his rifle range and his golf course. Every morning he blazes away there with a Morris Tube and drills a very pretty little pattern in his little white target. If the unfortunate animals which are at present browsing innocently in Tanganyika could see these patterns, they would experience a very uncomfortable sensation at the pits of their respective stomachs. After the shooting comes the smacking of golf balls into a net. For the benefit of others minded to experiment I should say that this is, in fact, a large garage which holds two cars: but it would do just as well if it were only half the size, since one of the cars remains there throughout the performance.

The garage is some thirty-four feet in length, and the width of it, which is used for golf, is no more than the width occupied by one not very large car. The net, moreover, is not at all an elaborate or expensive device, and is of amateur construction. The back wall and side walls, if I may so term them, are made up of a great variety of miscellaneous objects, such as might have come, as I thought, from those famous mounds of dust in Mr Boffin's garden. There were pieces of sacking padded with straw, and there were old mattresses, and there were rather mysterious iron railings, which appeared once to have been part of some kennels —the whole constituting a fine solid receptacle for any ball. The mattresses, of course, receive the ball's frontal attack, the railings act rather as buttresses. Originally there had been a piece of railing in the front wall, but one day a perverse ball lighted exactly on it and, despite all the straw and sacking, bounded back some thirty feet and hit the practiser a severe blow in the waistcoat. Finally, there is a net overhead and on each side attached to something in the nature of curtain rods, and the tee consists of a good, big board to which are affixed two mats, one for the ball and one for the player's feet.

The ceremony begins with the driving of one car into the mews outside. Next the nets are pulled out along their curtain rods. When he sees this being done, the Welsh terrier, which is always in attendance, knows what is going to happen, and retires to a position of safety under the other car. The tee is then placed in position; the chauffeur, with a huge basket full of balls, takes up his position on a low stool next door to it and, as one ball is driven off, tees up another. He struck me as a brave man. My friend, the owner of the garage, is one who wholly disdains a waggle. The moment a ball is there he hits it. Consequently, the chauffeur has to take his fingers away as quick as may be. Indeed, he puts the ball on the mat with something of the action of one placing the ball for a kick at goal in Rugby football. However, coal miners and steeplejacks and other people get used to the most perilous employments, and both he and the Welsh terrier appear to regard it as all in the day's work. There are some eighty balls in the basket and when the cease fire sounds it is pleasant to see the Welsh terrier emerge from under the car and stretch himself in safety.

A little while ago I was writing, in another place, of a gentleman who also had eighty balls teed up in a row, and then lashed them off as fast as he could to three little boys placed in the deep field. I said then it was very hard work, and I say it again now. Whether it is done in the open air or in a garage makes very little difference; it is the pace that kills. At golf schools, where there is much hitting into nets, the authorities have, I believe, decided that half an hour of it at a time is as much as any pupil can usefully endure: and I am not in the least surprised. It takes less than that to make my brain reeling and dizzy, and my hands, which I have always regarded as proof, uncommonly sore. Yet there is something very exhilarating about it. This game in a garage is something like a cross between golf and squash rackets. The inventor of it has the same motive which made the East India Sugar Broker in the Bab Ballads dance every day from Brompton to the City; he wants to get his weight down, and he could hardly have devised a better plan.

There is one small phenomenon that I have always observed in my own case in driving into a net. Perhaps other people have discovered it in theirs. I find that my follow-through is almost invariably of a far more chaste and classical character than it is on the links; my hands whirl round my head in the greatest style, and at the same time I have at the finish a certain amount of weight on my right foot. In short, because I am in no anxiety as to where the ball is going, I am in no hurry and so do not lurch forward with my body and get through too soon. Nor do I think that this is an exceptional case; other people playing into nets seem to me to finish far better than they do in real golfing life. The same thing often happens when we play golf so late at night that it is impossible to follow the flight of the ball. Once we realise that it is of no use looking, that the only hope of finding it lies in walking to where the ball ought to be, then we begin to follow through beautifully and to hit as straight as an arrow.

Jim Barnes, the American professional, has rather a good phrase by means of which he tries to teach his pupils not to hurry. He tells them 'not to think ahead of the shot,' to think about taking the club back when they are taking it back, not to let their mind skip forward to the moment of striking. I fancy that when we are hitting into a net we unconsciously follow this excellent piece of advice. To do it consciously on the links is a different matter. I wonder whether, if I had a chauffeur to tee my ball and a Welsh terrier to walk round with me, I could recapture the illusion.

KING CHARLES'S HEAD
(1926)

Anyone who discourses steadily on one subject becomes only too well aware that certain topics recur as constantly in his writings as did King Charles's head in Mr Dick's memorial. My particular King Charles's head is, as I know, Aberdovey. Yet, since I have been faithlessly absent from that course for three long years, I have been kept more or less silent about it for that time. Now I am on the eve of going back there. Indeed, I am writing rather early in order to be completely lazy when I am there. So now I can keep silence no longer. Snow or no snow, I am bubbling over with thoughts of returning, and must let myself go.

It *is* exciting to go back to the course where you played very nearly your first shot, where you first rose to the dignity of being a member of the club, where you had your first handicap and won your first prize. Those early prizes come back to my mind as a truly singular collection. Let me see what they were. There were two velvet razors in a blue velvet case. I was too young to shave with them, and shaved instead the horn at the bottom of my driver. That finished one of them.

Item the second: a silver candlestick (plated, no doubt) standing on crossed gold clubs and intertwined with a laurel wreath. This is believed still to survive in the family plate chest, but my eyes have not seen it for some while. Item the third: a card-case covered with a hideous floral design. Fate uncertain, but I hope and believe it is lost. Fourth, and silver hand-glass. Quite as useless as the razors, and, therefore, grudgingly and ungraciously given to a sister.

It seems to me that prizes have changed and one cannot win such curious things nowadays. At any rate, I do not. We changed later at Aberdovey and received mere sordid money orders instead. With an accumulation of these I bought myself an early edition of *Pickwick*, still much beloved. There was a horrid rumour as to another winner that he had spent his prize money on socks, an act of doubtful amateurism, but I hope it was not true.

The handicaps under which this miscellaneous assortment of articles was won were awarded, if I remember rightly, by popular vote. The competitors for the early meetings were few, so that we formed ourselves into a sort of Soviet and handicapped one another.

As to the course itself, I should have said it had changed very little. Then I began to go over it in my head and found that there are only four holes out of the whole eighteen which are now the same as when I played my razor-winning round. There is Cader, with its black-boarded sandhill. That is immortal and immutable, though the green is no longer the little 'pocket-handkerchief' that it used to be, and our ball may come kicking off the side walls where once it would have been deep in sand. Then there is the next hole, the Pulpit, with its imposing tee shot. True, the green is carried farther on, but the hole is essentially the same. There is the short hole at the end (is it now the ninth or tenth?), quite unchanged in one sense and wholly changed in another. Once the bunker was a real bunker, vast and yawning, and the sand was full of little bits of slate, and there was an overhanging black-boarded edge. Today the sand is grass-grown and the boards have been supplanted by a kindlier bank, and we can play it all too easily with an iron and get a four anyhow or nohow. With a gutty ball, a heavy cross-wind and a wooden club, that *was* a hole. When the great Braid came there he called it one of the very best of short holes, and he did not flatter it. Alas! its time has gone by and it is but the shadow of its old self. Finally, there is the sixteenth, still a great hole, with the railway on the left and the sandhills on the right. The cart ruts into which one hooks under the railway line are no longer six inches deep, but one cannot have everything. Another great hole by a railway line, the sixteenth at St Andrews, is easier than it used to be.

I really think it must have been rather an amusing and original place in those ancient days. Was there, I ask people from other places, ever another course where a poor lunatic gentleman dug a trench across the course to mark his record drive and it was left undisturbed? Where else were there crenellated walls to the bunkers like the battlements of a sham baronial castle? Where else were foursomes played against Colonel Bogey and Professor Goblin? I say nothing of the visitors having their matches made for them by the charming old lady who sold them their lunch, nor of their getting their lodgings from the secretary, their wine from the chemist, and their lessons in golf from the foreman of a timber yard. Neither, perhaps, is there anything very remarkable in the fact that the first photograph of the club represents the President taking his driver in Cader bunker to play in exactly the wrong direction, while his companions carry skates in their hands. Yet I have never seen such another photograph. I doubt if all or any of these things ever did happen anywhere else, and, sad to relate, none of them happens now at Aberdovey.

Even so, there is a thrill not quite like any other in going back there, as I know from the old premonitory symptoms, a perfect hatred of any work for two or three days beforehand and a ridiculously premature packing of my clubs. There are few changes nowadays in my bag of clubs, and when I start on any other golfing journey I just count them to see that I am not leaving my putter behind, and that is all. This time, however, I have already put two or three extra clubs into the bag, and then taken them out again. They are all old friends who have been there before, and it seems a shame not to let them have their outing. Moreover, one of them would be just the club for the Cader, I know. So I shall go on until the day comes.

When once I am fairly started a calm will settle down on me until I get to Shrewsbury. Shrewsbury is to Aberdovey what Leuchars is to St Andrews, Ashford to Rye, Minster to Sandwich. To be sure, it is a great deal farther off than any of them, but still, it plays the same part; it is the beginning of the last lap when the bell rings and we see with the mind's eye the tape ready to receive us. Once past Shrewsbury I shall begin to fidget, to count the wayside stations, to look out of the window, and the eerie cry of the newspaper boys at Moat Lane Junction—surely the most melancholy of all human sounds—shall 'sing me hame to my ain countree.'

LUNCHEON IS SERVED
(1927)

The Old Wellingtonians and the Old Cheltonians gave, between them, a few days since, a most instructive demonstration of the relations between golf and lunch. They played a match at Camberley Heath, by singles in the morning and foursomes in the afternoon. In the singles, Wellington were three up with four foursomes to play. No doubt they lunched with carefree minds, little knowing what was in store for them. Of defeat they can hardly have dreamed, but defeated they were, for Cheltenham won every single foursome, and so the match by a single point. I think it is tolerably safe to assume, having regard to the friendly nature of such matches, that all the players ate an equally good lunch. Therefore, we can only suppose that it had a remarkably different effect on the two sides, inspiring the one with a 'dormy' feeling, good-natured, relenting, a little comatose, and the other with a reckless, die-in-the-last-ditch courage.

If this is so, it accords with the individual experience of every one of us. Lunch is a fickle and capricious jade. We can never depend upon her favours. Sometimes she will rescue us from an abyss of woe; at other times she delights in proving to us that we are not playing half so well as we think. I hope that everyone knows the dear old picture in the

Badminton volume called *The Man to Back*. The gentleman depicted is supposed to have tied for a medal in the morning, and to be now fortifying himself before going out again to play off the tie. In front of him is a large pie dish which he has entirely emptied of its contents, and he is draining a glass of champagne, tilted well over his nose. Mr Hutchinson tells us that we may go out and back him with a light heart as opposed to the man whom we see 'toying with a biscuit and a lemon and soda.' Probably, he is right, although I never remember to have seen him carrying out his own precepts at the luncheon table, but there would be a good many exceptions to prove his rule. I know one golfer, a sober, godly and righteous person, who was tempted to follow this advice in an Amateur Championship, and the result was disappointing, for he lost the first four holes in succession. He was ultimately beaten on the eighteenth green, and it is open to the champagne school of thought to say that he would never have been able to make so gallant a spurt if he had lunched less well. The other side would certainly take the point that he would not have lost the first four holes on a different regimen, and they seem to me to have the better of the argument.

The real fact is that circumstances alter cases, and the man who has scraped through his morning round at the nineteenth hole wants a better lunch than he who has won by 5 and 4. I remember one big professional match, a good many years ago now, in which lunch played an important part. It was a seventy-two hole match, and with the last round to go, one player was three or four down. This did not prevent him from lunching heartily, almost jovially; he topped his first tee shot into a bunker in front of his nose, and appeared exceedingly amused at the circumstance. His more ascetic adversary was filled with sorrow and shame for him, but his sympathy was misplaced, for the well lunched one, after being, I think, five down with thirteen to go, began to play tremendous golf, recovered hole after hole, and in the end won the match by two up and one to play.

A historic example of the good effects of a good lunch is to be found in Mr Hilton's *Golfing Reminiscences*, which I was re-reading the other day yet once again. It was in the Open Championship of 1897 at Hoylake. At the end of the first day Mr Hilton was one stroke behind the leader, Braid, but in his third round he frittered strokes away sadly, taking 84 without getting into a single hazard. This was, as he says, 'weak-kneed golf,' and for that kind of golf there is nothing like lunch; so he ate 'many good things' and finished up with trifle, because one of those who ministered to him told him that 'trifle was the finest thing in the world on which to do a 75.' And 75 he did, and won the Championship by a single shot. After that he must be a hardened sceptic who can disbelieve in second sight—or in second helpings.

As against that may be set a memorable instance of a small and quick lunch. In 1925 Mr Gillies won the Presidents' Putter at Rye, beating Mr Tolley in the semi-final and Sir Ernest Holderness in the final on one and the same day. He had begun his first match very late owing to the frost, and had won it only on the nineteenth green. Consequently, he had, to the best of my recollection, just a quarter of an hour's interval before starting again, and some of that scanty allowance he spent in changing his shoes and stockings. What he had for lunch I cannot now remember, but, assuredly, it cannot have been much. It must, however, have been full of vitamins, for he played like an angel in the final.

I suppose that everybody has his own little private beliefs or even superstitions in this matter. For myself I always feel that a large cigar after lunch is in the nature of a kill or cure remedy. It seems to induce a pleasing sleepiness, an impression that it does not much matter what happens at the first hole or two. That may be beneficial or detrimental, but it involves the taking of a risk. It would be very agreeable to be able to smoke cigars—long, black ones—all the way round, as Mr Travis used to do, but that is a height to which few can aspire. Probably, nobody ever laid down for himself rules about smoking at golf without instantly breaking them. The rule I should like to be able to make is to light up only when things are going well. With the converse rule, every bad shot is apt to mean a cigarette, and there are so many bad shots.

Whether we lunch modestly or prodigally, we all get fits at times of believing that we play better either before or after lunch and, naturally, the more we dwell upon it the more our belief is likely to prove true. I knew one golfer who was so convinced of his own relative superiority after lunch that on the morning of a match he would resolutely turn breakfast into lunch, and finish up with cheese and coffee and a glass of port at ten o'clock in the morning. This, I am disposed to think, was showing too much zeal. His second lunch must surely have proved a disappointment.

ACES OF CLUBS
(1928)

A golfing friend of mine announced quite suddenly at luncheon the other day that he had lost many matches because his opponent possessed better clubs than he did; indeed, he was convinced that nearly all his defeats were attributable to this cause. The others of us believed this to be merely a sally of sparkling exaggeration, but he added, with marks of the most serious concern on his face, that, try as he would, he never, never could buy a good or even a decent club.

This seemed curious, as he is, in other walks of life, as I should judge, something of a connoisseur who would choose with deliberation, discretion and success. It is, however, an undeniable fact that comparatively few people have an eye for a club. I know that I have not got it, for, though I can now and again acquire a club which I like myself, nobody else ever likes it—a state of things reassuring as regards theft, but otherwise humiliating. In order to console our friend we all, there and then, declared ourselves to be wholly incompetent in the choosing of clubs. Especially did we say that which is quite true, that in a big shop away from the links the mind grows hopelessly dizzy with looking at clubs, and the wrists lost all sensation with waggling them; the mere fact of soling a club not on turf, which is its natural element, but upon wood or linoleum, seems to have some subtly disastrous effect, so that we are capable of buying a club either far flatter or far more upright than is our normal pattern. One shrewd person declared that he never bought a club unless he were allowed to take it for a trial round in his bag on sale or return. Various other pieces of good advice were proffered, but the best was the last. 'After all,' said somebody, 'So-and-so's way is really the only one. When he sees a good club in another man's bag, he just puts it in his own.' 'Yes,' added a still more defamatory somebody else, 'and changes the grip in case it should be identified.'

I am not, personally, afraid of So-and-so. Nobody (touching wood and in a good hour be it spoken) steals my clubs, just as I truly believe myself not to have stolen anyone else's, but I have known what it is to lose a favourite iron, and it is for the moment, and sometimes for a long while, a sad blow. I doubt whether it is a blow that befalls people as often as it once did, not because there is a higher level of honesty in the clubhouse, but because there are not so many long-treasured irons as there were. Indeed, I have just been reading somewhere in an American magazine an article saying that the favourite (spelt, of course, without its u) club is disappearing. If this be so, it is due to those elaborate series of matched and numbered irons with which everybody plays today. There are five or six of them in a set, all bearing so strong a family resemblance to one another that it seems hardly possible for the owner to conceive a wild passion for any particular one of them. Not long ago I was watching a golf match, and there was among my fellow-watchers one who should, but for a recent and, as I trust, temporary lapse of form, have been playing in it. To console himself and regain hope he had bought a beautifully matched set, and as he watched he dandled one of them

—number three or four or five. He did so with an air of genuine affection, and I sincerely hope it will serve him well, but it can never be quite what a unique and favourite iron once was; it has too many sisters that will do almost as well.

The favourite club of an older generation was, as a rule, a servant of all work. It had one main function, of course, but it also had several subsidiary ones, and it was often called on to perform one of these at an extreme crisis. It was, let us say, what was once called a driving iron and would today be called a 'No. 2.' It chiefly drove, but it had on occasions pitched, especially against a wind, it constantly ran up and, once or twice, when the putter had gone obstinately on strike, it had come nobly to the rescue and had scuffled two or three putts of most crucial length into the hole. Probably, it had also taken part in some one-club matches which had put money into its owner's pocket. So it was an old and trusted friend 'well tried through many a varying year,' and its owner, conscious that orthodoxy demanded some other club for a particular stroke, had yet often said, 'No, hang it, give me the old one. I feel safer with that.'

As time goes on there will be fewer and fewer such clubs as that, except in the corners of lockers or, perhaps, suspended honourably upon the wall. For the sake of pure skill it is, probably, a good thing that there should be fewer. It is difficult not to work a favourite club a little too hard; we take it because we know we can make some sort of a respectable stroke with it, and thus put off and off the hour of learning to play the shot with the right club. A favourite driving mashie may be bad for its owner's brassie play, a pitching mashie may render atrophied his half-iron shot, and so on. Moreover, a favourite is often a club of such strong and peculiar character that it is impossible to get any others like it; it makes all the other irons in the bag feel a little strange and uncomfortable. I have never possessed matched quadruplets or quintuplets, but the advertisements tell me that, if I did, I should not be able to tell one from the other with my eyes shut. I should swing them all in just one way and play the same old shot, sometimes with one and sometimes with the other, for ever and ever. If I were some years younger and could learn to do it, what a much better iron player I might be; but, ye gods! how dull!

As it is, my set of irons, though I am not conscious that they quarrel very violently among themselves, certainly do not bear any close or obvious relationship to one another; I cannot think that they are even the most distant of cousins. My so-called driving iron, bought for somebody else and then—well, not stolen, but gradually re-absorbed into my bag—is a perfectly straightforward, ordinary iron, but while other people would have a 'No. 3' of the same type, I have a 'jigger,' with a shallow face and a bulging back-view, of an entirely different pattern. Then after that comes a mashie without a heel, built according to the prescription of Mr G. F. Smith. The mashie-niblick also has a kink in its neck, so, I suppose, these two may be considered related. Generally speaking, however, they must be admitted to be a job lot. It is, of course, open to anyone to infer that I should play better if they were not.

PS—On re-reading this article I find I have told a lie, and, like George Washington, I can't. I did once steal a golf club, but it was only from the Red Cross, and we all stole things in wartime, and I did want it so very badly. I still have it now, and for ten whole years I have been meaning to play just one stroke with it again, and have postponed the attempt. It was so great a favourite once that I dare not risk the disillusionment.

REGRETS FOR BURIED TIME
(1929)

There cannot be in the world a golfer of so serene and sunny a temperament that he has no haunting regrets about the game. I do not mean merely as to particular shots and putts which, had they been holed, might have won for him monthly bogey competitions or amateur championships, but those of a more general character, regrets for some little piece of invaluable knowledge which has, as he bitterly believes, come too late.

There is an old friend of mine, not quite so young as he was, but still a very fine golfer, as he has recently shown. For years he was a bad putter, or, at least, if not nearly so bad as he thought, not a very good or trustworthy one. Nowadays he putts well, and he attributes this entirely to the fact that, whereas he used to putt with hands well out from his body, he now has them tucked in. If he had made this discovery years ago, the history of golf might have been changed, but, as he says with unconscious pathos, 'Nobody ever told me.'

It sets one thinking as to what might have happened to other eminent players if only somebody had told them in the days of their youth. Suppose, for instance, a good many years ago now a kind friend had taken away Mr Edward Blackwell's putting cleek and broken it, and insisted on his using the aluminium club with which today he is so admirable and consistent a putter. He would have needed, to be sure, to be a big, bold friend as well as a kind one, for Mr Blackwell is not the person with whom I should personally choose to take such liberties; but still, suppose there had been somebody wise enough and brave enough, the roll of our champions would very likely have been different from what it is now. Or suppose, to take another alarming person, somebody had told Edward Ray, when he was a boy, to keep that large body and those large feet of his just a little stiller, would he not have been even greater than he is? And what of the good Samaritan somebody who might have seized the right elbow of the juvenile Mr Horace Hutchinson and forcibly held it down? Whether he could have made Mr Hutchinson a better player than he was is doubtful; that is a good deal to ask, but he might indirectly have made better players of some other people who have read the beloved *Badminton*.

Let me give an even more exalted example than any of these. In Mr John Low's delightful book, *Concerning Golf*, which is now more than a quarter of a century old, there is a chapter on the art of driving by Mr Hilton. In it he alludes to the fact that Harry Vardon 'takes the club up vertically but brings it down with a horizontal sweep.' He adds that he 'thanks a beneficent Providence for not superadding to Vardon's wonderful powers of clean hitting and accurately judging distance, and to his perfect temperament for the game, an opportunity of acquiring early in life the one piece of scientific knowledge which would have made him absolutely invulnerable.' I wonder whether those thanks to Providence were not wasted and whether Harry Vardon could have played better. He might have putted better certainly; but driven better—I can hardly conceive that.

Being sprung from a scientific family, I am by no means convinced that scientific knowledge would have made him better; it might have made him worse. It is more cheering to think so, because then the knowledge that has come too late to the rest of us may not, after all, be so valuable as we imagine.

We all, however humble, have our regrets, and one of mine is that I was not coached in my youth. And yet it might have done no good. I recollect very well that on one occasion, when I was a small boy at Felixstowe, my father asked Thompson, the professional, to look at my swing. So he looked, and he said, very properly, that I was too flexible at the knees. I tried to amend my ways, but I have not even now succeeded in amending my knees; indeed, I have long since given them up as a hopeless job. So, in a sense, it is less depressing to believe that I was past praying for from the very first. I have another regret from those early days. I wish I had been given a putter and had not been allowed to scramble or scuffle the ball into the hole with a lofting iron—a feat, by the way, which years ago I could perform by no means unsuccessfully. In my bitter day-dreams I see myself, as I should have been if I had been given that putter, standing graceful and erect and hitting the ball a free, firm, confident blow. But in my heart I know that it is only a dream, and that I was born a croucher and a scuffler. There is a certain measure of miserable satisfaction in that knowledge.

There is another regret of mine which I dare say a good many other people share with me in hot weather. I wish I had learnt to play in my shirt-sleeves. It is not that I am too proud or too conservative and have not really tried. Some of my very earliest recollections of myself are of playing in nothing whatever but a flannel shirt, with no tie and no collar stud, and a very scanty pair of shorts—a costume which would delight the Men's Dress Reform League, of whose activities we now read so much. As far as I remember, I did very well, and it was probably at a later and more self-conscious stage of development that I came to believe myself unable to do it. Today, at least, the belief is all too well founded. I tried hard to learn it in wartime, for no man can play in 'jacket officers one,' if that be the right description, and in a temperature of a hundred and something in the shade. Yet it was a failure, and I never felt thoroughly comfortable till once more attired in (I shall again try to use something like military language) 'Jacket, Civilian Grey Flannel, 1914 pattern (obsolescent). Unserviceable.' The first time I swung my club again in that jolly, dirty old coat really brought home to me what I had suffered in the war.

Since then I have just given up the attempt, sweltered and done my best, but I think that any golfer who is reasonably young and does not learn to play in his shirt-sleeves is being exceedingly unwise. A fortnight ago in a match at Sunningdale I saw the foursome behind mine all in shirt-sleeves well rolled up, and was not in the least shocked, only envious. There was some consolation in the fact that they played ill, but that was not due to the shirt-sleeves. There was, as the famous Mr Sutherland would have said, 'too much levity' about that foursome. And even that fact brought its envies and regrets. I lamented that nobody had told me that golf would make me very unhappy and that I had far better not play it.

DEAD STRAIGHT
(1930)

I have a friend who knows a great deal about golf; a man, on the whole, of a kindly disposition, but something of a cynic. Whenever we meet and talk, he ends by saying, 'Well, now I have given you material for two or three articles.' Perhaps he exaggerates a little his own capacity for making illuminating statements, or mine for that expansion sometimes called by a less charitable name. However, I am not ungrateful to him, because on this last occasion he, at any rate, gave me a start.

We were discussing the seventeenth hole on the new course at Addington, which most people think is the hardest short hole in the world. There is one perfectly obvious reason for its hardness in the fact that the green is exceedingly narrow. On that particular day my opponent and I had, by a miracle, both stayed on the green, I only an inch from the drop on the left-hand side and he some four feet from the bunker on the right; yet the distance between our two balls did not look more than a dozen yards or so. My learned friend, however, gave me a much subtler reason than this; it was not his own, but that of Abe Mitchell, who had lately been playing there. The great Abe had said that if the tee were moved a little to the right or a little to the left, people would be getting their threes gaily enough; what beat them was the fact that it was a dead straight shot. I am sure that this was a sound piece of observation. Are not the shots that frighten us most those in which teeing-ground, fairway and putting green are in an exact straight line? When we shoot at the fairway from an angle, whether from the right or the left, we feel far less frightened. We take up our stance naturally and we hit the ball. When we must go straight our feet begin instinctively to wriggle, we feel that we want to aim a little to one side or the other; to aim right down the middle makes us feel cramped and uncomfortable. Many people know the long fifteenth at Woking called 'Harley Street.' Once upon a time it was worthy of its name, and everybody went crooked; now the rough comes with a curve into the middle of the course on one side, and the heather is cut back in a curve on the other; result, nobody thinks the hole a very difficult one, and fives are as common as need be.

The reason why the shot played at an angle is an easier one I take to be something like this: that we feel we have more room to manœuvre in. It seems that we can aim out rather farther to the left and allow for a slice (shall we call it, more politely, a drift?), or to the right and allow for a draw. This 'feeling'—and the whole business is one of that cursed thing imagination—makes all the difference in the world. Let us take another example, from a hole at which there is an 'out-of-bounds' on one side or the other. I was reading the other day in one of Vardon's books and he remarked, 'If you have an out-of-bounds area on either the right or the left, it is surely a sound idea to make your tee as far as possible from that evil region.' That sounds unimpeachably good sense, and it is probably quite right from the point of view of making the ideal shot, but I respectfully doubt whether it is good advice for the ordinary weak-minded golfer. Personally, if I have an out-of-bounds on my right, I tee my ball rather on the right-hand side of the teeing ground, because thus I feel I have more room; I can aim at a point in the air a little farther to the left. It is a confession of weakness; I realise that I might hit a longer shot from the left-hand side of the teeing ground, but I am more likely to hit a safe and respectable shot from the right-hand side, and I am inclined to believe that this is sound psychology as regards the average person.

The impish tricks of this sort that our imagination can play us are numberless. Here is another that occurs to me. Suppose we have to play an approach shot of moderate length and there is a bunker between us and the hole; we have to pitch, and so we do pitch; we are not particularly frightened, we play the shot tolerably well, perhaps we carry the bunker and make the ball sit down somewhere on the green. If there is no bunker in the way, can we play that shot in the same way? 'Not,' as the Americans might say, 'on your life.' We play some kind of a nondescript, scuffling stroke, not necessarily because we are fond of it, and not altogether because there is thus less chance of a complete foozle, but because we 'feel' that we cannot pitch unless there is something to pitch over. This is not so with the professional. He has, as a rule, made his pitch shot so mechanical that he can reproduce it irrespective of circumstances. Sometimes he seems a little too mechanical in this respect, and pitches when it would be more profitable to run; but still, his fault is on the right side, and, on the whole, he simplifies and makes the game easier for himself.

There is something to be done in such cases by a treatment in the nature of a counter-irritant. Let me give an egotistical instance. At my old friend Aberdovey the third hole is 150 yards or 160 yards long, there is a big sandhill to carry, and the green is rather of the kindly, soup-plate variety with banks that turn the ball inwards towards the hole. To a reasonably competent player it is a very easy shot. If, on some other courses, at 150 yards from the hole I can say to myself, 'Now just think you are playing Cader,' I can often produce an extremely creditable high pitching shot. This recipe is not always successful, but it sometimes is. One of a similar kind might, I am sure, be very useful to those who are apt to come through in front of the ball and so smother their shots. Let them picture to themselves with all the force of their imagination a mighty hill towering in front of them. I do not promise them that they will not go digging too much with the right shoulder, and so perhaps slice, but they will give themselves, I believe, a reasonable chance of waiting for the ball and they will not smother it. Proceeding on these principles, I presume that at that hole at Addington, which I took as my text, we ought to imagine that we have a crooked shot to play instead of a straight one. Yet somehow I doubt if that would be effective. Perhaps my learned friend will tell me next time.

OUT-OF-SEASON JOYS
(1931)

On the night when the Open Championship ended at
Carnoustie I crossed the Tay and made for St Andrews,
deeming it a crime to be so near and not have one day's golf
there before returning south. Fortune was cruel, and it
rained so hard that there was really nothing for it but to sit in
the club and look drearily through the big window. Out of
that window, usually so interesting a watch-tower, there was
very little to look at, for only two or three heroic ladies in
mackintoshes drove off the first tee. Yet even so, though I
raged at fate, there was something novel and exciting about
the experience, because I realised that, often as I had been to
St Andrews, this was the first time I had been there in more
or less of an off season, when the place belonged to itself and
not to me, the golfing tripper. The novelty was emphasised
as the day wore on, because at last, in despair, two companions and I went out, each with a club and two or three
balls, and slashed about between the clubhouse and the
burn, with nobody to object to us or get in our way.

My two companions, who lived at St Andrews, took it as a
matter of course, but to me there seemed something almost
sacrilegious about it. Never before had I dreamed of such a
thing. As a rule, when I want to practise at St Andrews I am
driven to the sea shore, which, except for occasional lovers,

dogs and motor-bicyclists, is not a bad place and agreeably flatters one's driving powers. Now here I was, practising on a spot which had always seemed to me as impossible for that purpose as, let us say, Trafalgar Square. What a miserable southern tourist I was, a mere member of a holiday rabble! It occurred to me that I had once had much the same experience at another famous links—Prestwick. I have, as a rule, been to Prestwick at a time of championships, and so have only made an intolerably slow progress round a course all too full both of players and onlookers. Yet just once I did go there on an off day and, behold, we had the whole of that noble expanse to ourselves and played a five-ball match with nobody in front and nobody behind.

I could say much the same of other great Scottish courses, and the moral is that many of us English are very foolish in not trying more resolutely to go to Scotland when all the rest of the world is not going there, too. There are, of course, excellent reasons—such tiresome things as time and work and money—but, still, there is something wrong in a state of things that connects Scottish golf in the mind with a struggle for a time and a struggle for a caddie. And I hereby register a vow that some time before I die I am going north at a season when other southern golfers are sticking to their desks, and then I shall have the most delightful golf of all my life. At the present moment I know of a happy band who have made a plan to go to St Andrews and play foursomes *after the medal is over.* They have suggested that I should go with them, but it sounds almost too good to be true: one of the dreams that will never be realised.

Nevertheless, it is very pleasant to indulge in hopeless day-dreams, and I amuse myself now and then with this one, wondering the while what it is that makes the thought of Scottish golf more exciting than that of any other kind.

Sometimes I think it is the burns that make the difference. Water hazards are not, so far as I know, particularly good things in themselves. There are some on English courses that give no gratification. I get no thrill from my ball sailing over or plunging into the Suez Canal at Sandwich, nor the brook in front of the first hole at Deal. I love Westward Ho! and I have a profound respect for the home hole there, but I do not love the Stygian drain that guards that green. On my best beloved Woking I have often put my second shot in a streamlet before the sixth green and topped into it again from the eighth tee, but I have no pleasure in the recollection and I call it not a stream but a ditch—with an epithet. Yet the moment the Scottish border is crossed a burn seems to be endued with magical qualities and no properly constituted course is complete without one. Moreover, it really is a burn, and there is no affectation in so calling it. The late Mr W. T. Linskill wrote of Coldham Common that 'its hazards are several burns,' but no one else at Cambridge had the splendid and un-selfconscious courage to use the term; 'ditches' faintly described them.

To be sure they have much better burns in Scotland than we have in England. The Swilcan at St Andrews may not be much to look at, and any impudent young Remus without a 'crocky' knee can jump over it, but it has done a lot of damage in its time and turned the issue of famous battles. I always think that a tablet ought to be put up on its banks recording how three great men, Mr Willie Greig, Mr Laurence Auchterlonie and Mr John Ball, all went into it at the nineteenth hole against Mr Leslie Balfour Melville when he won the Championship. Yet, if the best known, it is certainly not the greatest of burns. That honour should surely be given to the Barry burn at Carnoustie, which enjoys a justly enhanced celebrity since this year's Open

Championship. No mere English brook could wind itself in so complex a manner and guard so many greens at once. Either the tenth hole, 'South America, ' or the home hole would make the reputation of any ordinary burn, and this Barry burn makes both holes what they are and the seventeenth as well, where poor Jurado lost a championship in the 'black and dowie waters.' And then there is the Pow burn at Prestwick, which is the making of one of the greatest of all holes, the fourth, and also plays its part at the Cardinal and the Himalayas home. I have mentioned only three, but the list could be prolonged indefinitely. Lifting and dropping may be poor fun and poor golf, but a burn is a burn 'for a' that,' and in Scotland it is a noble and romantic hazard.

Then there is the matter of caddies. Some people like to hand themselves over body and soul to their caddies, but I am one of those vain and irritable creatures who do not like to be too sternly dragooned. By nature I prefer the silent English beast of burden to the imperious Scot. I have no evidence that the Scottish caddie can play better than I can the stroke on which he pours scorn; I am not convinced he knows more about the game and I do not relish his domineering manner. 'By nature' I repeat; yet when I go to a Scottish links I should probably feel a little disappointed if my caddie did not order me about and openly despise me. There would be a feeling that I might as well have stayed at home and that I was not getting my money's worth. There would be something lacking in the glamour and the atmosphere without this discipline.

I have ventured to suggest two reasons why Scottish golf is more romantic than any other, but, of course, everybody can best think of his own reasons, impalpable and inexpressible things, woven out of all manner of pleasant memories. Let me end by quoting something about it written in the

Cornhill some sixty-four years ago. 'There is a comfortable little club at St Andrews, which, like all the other institutions of the town, is subservient to golf. It stands at the end of the links, or downs, upon which the game is played, and from the windows, with a good opera glass, you can rake the first part of the course, and judge from the features and gestures of the players returning, whether they are losing or winning . . . The golfer, having finished a large and late breakfast, lights a cigar, and turns his steps towards the links and the club. Presently he is joined by another, and then another golfer, and about eleven o'clock little knots form in front of the club and in the parlour, and the process of matchmaking begins.' That is a delightful picture, though not quite a true one of 'the comfortable little club' in August and September nowadays, but when some day I take my dream-holiday there, perhaps it will be beautifully and exactly true.

RABBITS, TIGERS—AND SHEEP
(1932)

It is sometimes alleged by cynical persons that the middle classes can never band themselves together in defence of their rights and privileges because, when it comes to the point, nobody will ever admit that he belongs to the middle class. If this be a rule, I can, at any rate, produce one golfing exception to it, for I have just received an impassioned letter from a friend who openly proclaims that he is one of the golfing middle class and that they are most unjustly used. 'Do tell me,' he says, 'why all golf architects, golf writers and green committees divide golfers into two species, tigers and rabbits,' and he goes on to say that there is a third species—the vast majority of golfers, whom he calls, for the sake of brevity, sheep.

In any such discussion it is extraordinarily difficult to define our terms. What, for instance, constitutes a tiger? Personally, I should say that, leaving professionals out of account, an amateur tiger is one who is at least good enough to owe a stroke to scratch. He is also, in the common use of the term, a long driver. Indeed, today, when there is so much talk of length and so many people do hit a long way, we seem to be coming back to the notions of very ancient days when the world was divided into long and short drivers. Read the *Cornhill* article of 1867, which is to be found in Mr Clark's book, and you find all the arguing and bargaining at St Andrews, preliminary to the making of foursomes, presupposes a combination of the two different classes, the long and the short drivers. The long driver, though he was not then so named, was clearly the tiger, and the short was the rabbit. Some people will, no doubt, disagree with my definition, but they will not greatly disagree; so let us take the rabbit. What is his handicap and style of play? I should say that a man comes perilously near the rabbit class when he has a handicap of fifteen or so, but again considerations of length seem to obtrude themselves. A very steady old gentleman who hits very straight a very short way may play up to a handicap of twelve, but your scornful young slasher will unquestionably term him a rabbit, and he probably will not greatly resent it.

Between the two species, however exactly defined, there is clearly a large gap. My correspondent defines his 'sheep' who fills this gap as those with handicaps from four to fourteen. He goes on to say that it is difficult where to draw the line. There are steady-going middle-aged sheep in whom the only possible change is that their woolly fleeces will almost imperceptibly and painlessly turn into fur. About them there is no great difficulty, but there are, on the other hand, he says, 'those lusty lambs nearly full grown that can hit a ball out of sight and, although sheep, are obviously turning brown, growing claws and showing faint signs of stripes.'

My friend is not, however, merely concerned with these academic points, however interesting; he has a much more definite grievance, and here it is in his own words: 'The architect lays out a long hole, and says with a self-satisfied smile, "This is fine. The tiger can carry the hazard with two good shots, and the rabbit will get there nicely in three."

Yes, but what about the majority sheep? He drives, say, 210 yards down the middle, and there he is stuck. There is the green, 190 yards or 200 yards away, with a carry about 160 yards to 170 yards. He knows he can't do it. "Oh," say the architect and the Green Committee (the latter always jungle dwellers), "you are not meant to get there in two with a handicap of eight or ten. You must play short." What poisonous words! Drive a ball 210 yards down the centre of the fairway and then be told to play short, on the ground, I should add, that bogey is five!' Well, I agree with him that those last words are venomous indeed; in fact, I agree with him entirely that the situation he describes is wrong and inflicts at once undeserved tedium and hardship on the middle-class player. I do not quite agree with him, however, in thinking that this situation often arises today. Is he not going back to the days when Tom Dunn's ramparts used to rear their hideous heads right across the course? Then, if one could not go for the carry, there was nothing for it but to play short, and very dull it was; but nowadays the architect leaves, as a rule, a way open, though very properly a narrow way, through which the shorter hitter can pass—can 'sneak,' as the lordly tiger might say—if he is accurate enough. Why, even at the eighth hole at Woking our fine old crusted cross-bunker, the last of its race, has been taken away, and there is a road for wrigglers. However, I am nearly getting on to a grievance of my own, and shall desist.

I know the course on which my correspondent chiefly plays (no number of wild sheep shall drag its name from me), and there, I admit, he has some cause to complain. There are some holes, on that highly respectable course, where he must either go out, for England, home and beauty, to carry the grassy mountains with his second, or he must take an iron and play short, perhaps rather tamely. Yet even there this does not befall him so very often, and on most modern courses it scarcely befalls him at all.

For myself, there are certain holes at which I never mind having to play the sheep's game. There is, for instance, the fifteenth at Sandwich. When the tee is right back, I shall, most likely, have to play short in two; but then, the shot is not a really dull one, and can be played both well and ill. Moreover, the tiger who can get home in two must hit his shot accurately as well as far, or he may be much worse off than I am where I lie in my inglorious safety, short of the cross-bunker. In these circumstances it would be rather paltry and churlish of me to grudge him the advantage of his greater length. To have often to play short in such circumstances that 'any old shot will do' is utterly wearisome; but, on the other hand, the sheep ought to recognise that the hitting of a long, carrying second is a skilful feat and not merely attained by brute force.

There is another friend of mine, a wonderfully shrewd judge of golf, who would heartily applaud every word of my sheepish correspondent. I have often talked with him on this particular subject, but a cross-bunker to him is as a red rag to a bull, and, however tentative and diplomatic I try to be, he always ends by saying crushingly: 'You and I have different ideas of golf.' One particular bone of contention between us has been the Sea hole, the thirteenth, at Rye, which I hold to be a magnificent hole. He hates it, I shall not meanly say because he has to play short, but because the question of having to play deliberately short of the big hill does often arise. My contention is that this does not matter, because no amount of playing short can prevent the player —be he rabbit, sheep or tiger—having a difficult and interesting pitch at the last. When in a gracious mood he has gone so far as to admit that there may be something in this contention, but his lip curls in scorn nevertheless. You see, unfortunately, that pitch is a blind one; he disapproves of all blind shots; so that at this point we are apt to branch off into another fervorous argument on the general principles of golf. I really think I must try to introduce these two friends of mine to one another. They would get on like a house afire.

THE BLACK FLAG
(1933)

A kind correspondent has lately written to me about a golf match played for a unique stake, which could not offend those holding the most tremendous views on the wickedness of gambling. As a guarantee of good faith he has told me the name of one of the players, the course where they play, and the town where they live; but these, as Dr Watson used to say, 'for obvious reasons I suppress.'

Every Sunday these four players play two four-ball matches, in which the sides are always the same. No filthy lucre changes hands, but if either couple ever lose both matches they are bound under the most solemn oath to appear at their work on the following morning each wearing a black tie. So singular a vow has, naturally, not escaped the notice of their friends, who scan the Monday morning's neckwear of the combatants with the closest scrutiny, and if the black banner of defeat is seen it is hailed with heartless and uproarious merriment.

The case of the losers is fully as hard as that of our old friends of 1651, James Rodger, Johne Rodger, Johne Howdan and George Patersone, who were 'complained upon for playing at the golf upon ane Lord's day,' and, having confessed their 'prophaning,' were 'ordained to make their public repentance the next day.' No penitent, I am told, ever donned the white sheet with more sensible shrinking than they do their black, and they have even tried to avoid the extreme disgrace by the most transparent subterfuges, such as the putting on of a tie bearing the minutest white spots. Instant discovery has, however, always ensued, to be followed by the exaction of heavy though nameless penalties.

Black is obviously the right colour, in so far as it suggests mourning for lost holes, and yet I can conceive ties which might cause the wearers far greater agonies. As it is now, they are the victims only of their immediate circle. The ordinary citizen who sits opposite them in the train or passes them in the street is not a penny the wiser; but supposing they had to wear ties bearing a horribly garish combination of stripes, then everybody that met them would, as De Quincey said in *Murder as a Fine Art*, 'ogle their throats.' It is true that the said everybody would not know what they had done; he would only deem them insane, but that would be hard to bear. I have myself a drawer which is a moraine of ties ancient and modern. There are one or two that occasionally come to the surface, as I search feverishly for the one I want, and whenever I see them a shudder goes through me. There is one in particular that I ought to have worn when representing a distinguished club last year. By a strong effort I actually put it on, but I found that I really could not face my breakfast in it, and had to substitute something a little more peaceful. If those four golfers would like the recipe I shall send it them, and I can assure them that they will be glad to return to their present badge of defeat.

It would be interesting to have some statistics of how often this black flag has to be hoisted. Perhaps it is not very often. It may be that the pair who win in the morning are overcome by an agreeable 'dormy' sensation and luxuriate in their lunch accordingly, to the detriment of their afternoon's play. They may even feel sorry for the other side and let them off easily, but I scarcely think they do that; I believe, rather, that they apply themselves to the second round with a certain jovial malignity and a desire to have their prowess well advertised to their friends on the Monday morning. Here, however, I am only guessing, and that is a crime that as a schoolboy one was always told not to commit under the direst impositions.

How many matches these four golfers have played altogether, history does not record, but, at any rate, they still keep their reckoning by holes. I have heard of two old friends and regular opponents who thought holes too small and niggling a method of scoring and reckoned their gains and losses purely by matches. They played together nearly every day, and towards the end of the year the tension became great, since one or other of them might be five or six matches up with only twenty or so to play. To be dormy on the year's play was a glorious moment. In one year, if I remember rightly, one of the parties, finding himself a serious number of matches down, took a holiday, went to the seaside and had a series of lessons from a distinguished professional. Thus fortified, he came back and soon turned his deficit of matches into a profit.

In America golfers seem to have the habit of belonging to regular 'foursomes' (I am afraid they are really four-ball matches) and playing the same match together at weekend after weekend. If this habit is growing in England, then it may be the result of the motor car. This interesting piece of speculation is not mine, but belongs to Colonel A. N. Lee, who is this year the captain of the Notts Golf Club. He has revived the cheerful custom of a club dinner, which had fallen into desuetude since the war, and I had the pleasure of being a guest. In his speech Colonel Lee pointed out that in old days all the golfers went out to Hollinwell by one of two morning trains, according to their laziness or their industry, and returned by the same train in the evening. Thus everybody knew everybody else, and the man who had no match could pick one up in the train. Today everybody goes to golf in a car, and the same four players are apt to go and come back together, to the loss of general sociability. I had not thought of it before, but I expect he is right. No doubt the car is a blessed invention. Nevertheless, what fun it used to be, in dim ages past, going down to Woking in a slow and early train from Waterloo, stampeding down the platform at the other end for a good place in the wagonette, stampeding again up the path to the clubhouse to get a good place on the tee. The journey back, too, had its charms, even though the day was a very long one, and it was then that matches were made for the next weekend. Golf was a very sociable game then, or was it only that we were all rather younger and keener and pleasanter people?

That is a difficult question, but I have a very soft spot in my heart for those old train journeys in dear departed second-class carriages with such nice cheap tickets. Certainly I used to put on—metaphorically—a mournful black tie on the Monday morning when I thought that there were five or even five and a half days to be spent in an odious office before the journey and wagonette and the *sauve qui peut* rush for the tee came round again. Not even the two defeated ones of my story can ever have felt more thoroughly depressed. I do hope none of them will have to exhibit those dreadful symbols next Monday.

THE WINDS OF HEAVEN
(1934)

I was playing the other day with a perfectly good golfer. We
were coming to the Long Hole In, and he had hit a perfectly
good drive, well out of the reach of all the Beardies. He had,
unless I am mistaken, visions of carrying Hell with a superb
second, when—quite suddenly and unexpectedly—he
missed the globe. There was a mighty swing, the club
whistled through the air, and the ball remained *in statu quo*.
Was it a practice swing, or had the incredible thing really
happened? The rest of us hardly knew what to do, whether
to laugh or, pityingly, to avert the eye. After he had had
another shot and topped the ball some distance, one of us
asked him politely whether he had played three, and he
blushingly admitted the impeachment. It was a remarkable
feat; and let nobody think he was a beginner. On the
contrary, he has a handicap of six or so, which could very
soon be reduced. Moreover, did he not—confound him!
—win the match for his side at the crucial moment by doing
two admirable and consecutive fours at the Corner of the
Dyke and the Road hole?

He missed the globe in the fullest and most glorious sense
of the words, since he struck nothing but the winds of
heaven. I am never sure whether we are entitled to say that
we have performed that feat when our club strikes the

ground before passing over the ball. It all depends on what the coiner of the phrase meant by the term 'globe.' Was he alluding to the round earth, or did he use the word as a synonym for ball, in the same way that the sporting reporter used to talk of 'planting the leather between the uprights'? Personally, I prefer the first alternative, but I am afraid I must be wrong.

In search of an authoritative pronouncement I looked up the glossary at the end of the *Badminton* volume, and there found: 'Missing the globe. To fail to strike the ball either by swinging right over the top of it, or by hitting the ground behind.' If that be right, then I am wrong, but I shall always stick to my view that the only genuine and dramatic air shot is one in which the club meets nothing but air. A highly distinguished friend of mine, who has played for his county, was known for some while among the Deal caddies as 'the blighter that hit the air shot,' but I maintain he had not fully earned the title. I saw the stroke—in the Halford Hewitt Cup; his ball lay on an up-slope of one of the hills at the fifth hole, and it remained there in precisely the same place after he had done, but his club struck the ground. Similarly, I should like to be able to say that I once missed the globe on the first teeing ground and then won a scratch medal. In the *Badminton* sense it would be true. We played for the scratch medal at Cambridge on frozen snow, and I may charitably assume that I slipped on that first tee. At any rate, the ball did not move, but my driver head was covered with snow. I cannot claim the real distinction. I did not 'swing right over the top' of the ball. To do so is, in fact, for a golfer of any experience, a comparatively rare achievement.

That it should be so always seems to me one of the standing wonders of golf. The ball is so very small, and the clubhead is not very large. It is surely remarkable that they make contact so regularly. At lawn tennis we—I mean players of my humble class—are perfectly familiar with the sensation of having a hole in the middle of the racket, and at cricket the most eminent constantly miss the ball. Prosaic and laborious persons will no doubt explain to me that in these cases the ball is moving and that in golf it is stationary. Still, the thing remains to me a minor source of astonishment, and one day, towards the end of last month, at St Andrews, at eight o'clock in the morning, when the rain was coming down mercilessly and I had not had my breakfast, it seemed a positive miracle. I cannot help thinking, however, that that ball was not a globe at all. It reminded me, even in the moment of agony, of Mr Mantalini's words: 'The Countesses had no outlines at all, and the dowager's was a demd outline.' This ball had the demdest, vaguest, fuzziest outline and anybody might have missed it.

So far I have been talking of missing the globe with a full swing, but it attains, perhaps, the quintessence of poignancy as a spectacle when it is done in a short shot. There was an old friend of mine, now dead, who was prone to do it quite close to the hole. He was afflicted with a quick, nervous jerk, afflicted so badly that he came to eschew playing matches and preferred solitary practice. Even then he was not immune, and I have more than once seen him pass high over the ball with his mashie, cast a hasty look round to discover if there was any other eye upon him but his Maker's, and then pick the ball up casually and walk on.

Most of us have at some time or other jabbed our putters into the ground and left the ball motionless; but to pass clean over the ball on the green is rarer. I saw it happen once in the case of an agitated young subaltern, who had just joined his regiment and had to play in a foursome with a major. On the very last green, under the clubhouse windows, with everything depending on the hole, he left the ball severely alone; he must have missed it by a good six inches. Taking everything into consideration, I think that was the finest and most flawless example of the air shot that I ever saw. To be sure, it was not long ago that I played behind a man who made four consecutive air shots through the green; but he must have been a beginner, and beginners are not eligible for championships in this business of globe-missing; their advantages are too great. Neither can we consider the feats of Members of Parliament opening a new local course in their constituency, nor of Mayors who attempt a stroke in their robes and chains. In point of fact, I only once saw a Mayor open a course, and then it was a putting course. He holed a good long putt of several yards, and I can only say, as Jasper Petulengro did of the Bow Street runner, 'I am of opinion, brother, that Mayor must have been a regular fine fellow.'

NOT CRICKET, BUT . . .
(1935)

A kind friend gave me at Christmas a delightful little present, a book of Mr Horace Hutchinson's that I had never seen before. It is not a book about golf, but about cricket; is called *Cricketing Saws and Stories*; and was published in 1889 at the modest price of one shilling (5p). It is quite short, some fifty small pages in all, and is illustrated in that peculiar and engaging form of drawing, if it may so be termed, in which Horace excelled. He used it for depicting golfers as well as cricketers, and could show some players' trick of style, so that all his friends would recognise him, by means of four or five lines and a little round blob of ink for the head. Those who know and cherish the old volumes of the *Golfing Annual* will recall one of these little golfing men of Horace's—golden on a green ground—adorning the outside.

This little cricket book is, I believe, long since out of print, which makes my copy the more precious but is otherwise a pity, because the book has a gentle and characteristic humour which many people would enjoy. As I read it I translated a good deal of it, half unconsciously, into terms of golf, and reflected that cricketers and golfers were not very different under their skins and suffered from much the same amiable little weaknesses and vanities.

Take, for instance, the fifth 'saw' in the book: 'The bowling never looks so easy as just after it has proved itself sufficiently difficult to get us out.' That can be translated into golfing terms, I think, in one of two ways. Let us first consider how absurdly easy the course and the weather appear on a medal day just after we have torn up our card. The greens are of a perfect pace, there is not a breath of wind, the course playing very short because of the run in the ground—why, it scarcely seems credible that any being erect upon two legs could take more than 75. And yet that card of ours now floating on the breeze would have recorded something like 95, if it had been allowed. Or again, is there ever so palpably contemptible a golfer as the man who beat us in the first round of a tournament when we watch him playing in the second? He is perfectly ludicrous; he will infallibly be beaten by 7 and 6; a child could do it—and yet he beat us.

Here is another saw which somehow seems to remind us of our golfing selves: 'In most cases the man who has scored freely has a far higher opinion of the quality of the bowling than the man who has made a duck.' We often praise the tremendously powerful driving, the approaches ruled on the pin, the deadly putts of our late opponent, and then, in answer to the desired question, say airily: 'O, I beat him by 2 and 1.' On the other hand, the man who beats us we are prone to describe as a miserable scuffler with no shots and no swing, who won only because we took the match in both hands and hurled it at him. There are exceptions to this rule in the shape of those players who invariably credit their conquerors with superhuman achievements. Indeed, there are golfers of whom it is said that they have never been beaten by a man who took more than 69 to go round. Superficially, it seems the more generous weakness to invent wonderful feats for the man who beat us, and yet I doubt if generosity has much to do with it.

Here is another pleasant little saw with a golfing application: 'Should the batsman be defeating the bowling by means of any special style of stubborn defence or fearless hitting, it is the habit of some wicketkeepers to compliment him, in a tone of friendly interest, upon this feature of his play. This will in some cases produce on the batsman's part a slight self-consciousness which may aid his downfall and possibly turn the balance of the match.' When that was written there had been no talk of impairing the enemy's morale by propaganda, but the underlying principle was known to golfers before the war. The two methods which the unscrupulous generally use consist in praising the length of the enemy's driving or the deadliness of his putting. In the first case the victim blushes with gratified vanity and then begins to feel that he must live up to this newly acquired reputation as a mighty driver. He hits harder and harder, possibly, for a while, with success. Sooner or later, however, the insidious poison will begin to work; first he will lose his balance from his exertions, next he will lose his confidence, and finally he will lose the match.

The desired end will come still more swiftly and surely in regard to putting because putting is for most of us so very self-conscious a business. We live in a state of discarding old dodges and inventing new ones, and our red-letter day is that on which the newest dodge has not yet begun to wear out. Having had bitter experience before, we try not to think about it too much; but if our enemy flatters us into telling him of its virtues we shall not be able to help thinking about them. Some golfers, and very fine golfers, too, have even been temporarily destroyed by being asked to show an innocent enquirer how they hold their club. The greatest amateur that this country has produced has been known to refuse such a request from a hero-worshipper on the ground that he has been 'had that way before.'

Here is a piece of advice which may be useful when we want to be angry with our partner in a foursome for missing a very short putt: 'As captain, temper your criticism on the dropping of a catch by the consideration that in all probability by far the most vexed man in the field is he who has been the chief agent in the catastrophe.' And, finally, here is a small bit of philosophy rather appropriate at this season, when the coming of another New Year forces on our attention the melancholy fact that, far from improving at golf, we are getting worse. 'One of the most tranquillising and blessed truths,' wrote H. G. H., 'that can come home to a cricketer is his recognition of the sad fact that he has no talent for bowling.' If we could apply that maxim to our golf we should, I suppose, cease once and for all to be annoyed at being out-driven, and concentrate our placid minds on keeping down the middle of the course. We should, without a pang, play short of the bunkers that we used to carry with an iron shot. We should accept the annual raising of our handicaps with a gentle pleasure, and not be in the least disturbed by receiving strokes from those to whom we once gave them. In short, we should be entirely sweet and reasonable creatures, model partners and model opponents. We must try to attain to this blessed state in the coming year, but it is hard work.

DOWN MEMORY LANE
(1936)

The keeping of a diary is a matter on which people are as a rule rather reticent. Perhaps they are merely afraid of being thought to be bores who will pitilessly inflict pages of trivialities on their friends, and that is an admirable motive. Perhaps they cherish the hope that when they die they will blossom into an unexpected and posthumous fame as so many Pepyses. Whatever their reason, they are generally shy about admitting to anything of the kind, and so it happens that I have no notion how many of my friends keep golfing diaries and in how many books is some such entry as this: 'Beat B. Darwin by 6 and 5. He was perfectly hopeless, but I played rather well.'

I once kept a diary, and I wish I had gone on. Why I gave it up I hardly know, save that I reached the end of one book and, just as I was going to begin another, I had such a devastating and disastrous time on the links that I could not bear to record it. I solemnly and sincerely advise other people to keep one, not because it will necessarily become an historic document, but because just once or twice a year, a good many years hence, it will give them a sudden thrill to look at it, just as once in a very long while we enjoy turning up some ancient collection of stamps or the picture books of our childhood. My one day comes about Christmas time because—it is a shameful confession—I generally find there is not enough to do on Christmas Day. When all presents have been given and received and looked at and thanked for, when you have eaten your turkey and plum pudding and taken a walk to get rid of some of their effects, there is still time to spare, and it is then that I retire surreptitiously to my room and read my old diary with a certain melancholy pleasure.

This diary of mine began in 1899 and ended in 1903, so that I can look back at my matches of—to take a good round number—thirty-five years ago. One thing that strikes me in the retrospect is that while I have, of course, clean forgotten most of the games recorded, I have hardly forgotten a single one of my partners or opponents. It is only at very long intervals that I have to scratch my head and say: 'Snooks—who the deuce was Snooks? Anyhow, he can't have been much good, since I had to give him a half'; or else: 'Snooks must have been a good player, since he seems to have beaten me pretty comfortably—only, who the devil was he?' Almost the only occasions on which I have to puzzle my head over Snooks are those of a single visit to a course previously unknown to me. Then I imagine that he was the captain of the local club, and perhaps I may be pardoned for having forgotten him. At Aberdovey or Woking or Chiswick or Mid-Surrey or some other course on which I played regularly during those four years, I find no Snookses; I can remember all my opponents, sometimes vaguely and sometimes quite clearly, even down to the eccentricities of their respective swings. The mere writing down of their names in the book must have helped to grave them on my memory, and that is one advantage of keeping a diary.

Incidentally, how the writing does change from page to page during four years! It was not that my handwriting (many printers would deny that it deserved to be so called) was in a state of flux during that period. It is rather that the writer's mood changed constantly. When I see a beautifully neat and tidy page I feel pretty sure that things were going well with me, and that I enjoyed recording every night the modest triumph of the day. I am the more sure of this when I examine the page carefully and see that it is dotted here and there with nice little scores in nice little brackets with plenty of fours and threes and not too many sixes. There are, on the other hand, pages on which the doings of five or six days were clearly recorded at one and the same time. The writing becomes hurried and slovenly; there are no tidy little scores and only one or two despairing comments such as 'Driving unspeakable' or 'Putting too awful.' Then I know that, as one day of bad golf followed another, I put off each night the task of setting down the results, until at last, being forced to do my duty, I did it as perfunctorily as possible.

One would think that after thirty-five years defeat would have lost its bitterness, whereas the pleasure of victory would remain, but I am not sure that this is so; *surgit amari aliquid* even to this day. The reason is, perhaps, that I am, as I read, in the position of one knowing the future. As I see some good score, evidently recorded with pride and gratification, I know that it was but a flash in the pan; far from inaugurating a new and happier epoch, it was, in fact, the precursor of some major disaster. There is one springtime, for instance, towards the end of the gutty era, when everything appears rosy-coloured. It begins at Aberdovey, and there is a flamboyant entry followed by exclamation marks: 'Great field day. Three pots in one day.' When I look at it now I only say: 'Ha ha, my boy, you didn't know what was coming to you.' The calamity does not come at once. On the contrary, I proceed to St Anne's and, according to my statement, equal the amateur record, but as I had not a card and pencil this was very likely a lie. Once more at the present moment I laugh cynically, but at the time it was 'all wery capital,' and the entry that follows at Formby is cheerful enough. Then the page turns over; I get to Hoylake and suffer a complete collapse and a horrible double-figure defeat. What a good thing it is that the future is hid from us!

While a great many of the entries fail altogether to revive the memory, others stimulate it to an extraordinary degree. The sight of a particular patch of handwriting makes me remember exactly what new style or dodge I was cultivating at the time. It may be that the fine nib brings back the temporary triumph over an elbow or the fact that I was crouching less than usual; the fat nib suggests visions of a particular wooden club with a yellow head, and a dreadful fit of tumbling backwards, even without the note 'Something must be done about this driving.'

There are some pages, again, that strike me dumb with admiration at my own and my companion's energy, or perhaps I should rather say, with envy of our youth. Some six and thirty years ago I was staying at the same hospitable house by the same course from which I have but lately returned, and I find that for five consecutive days we played not only two singles each day but a nine-hole foursome afterwards. Just think how early we must have started to play five and forty holes on a January day, how quickly we must have walked and lunched, and, even so, how dark it must have been when we finally holed out. Just think, too, any of you who know the scene of those labours, that we had a very steep hill to climb afterwards, with no cars to carry us back after our one round as we have now. However, if I go on in this sad strain I shall induce people not to keep diaries, whereas I set out to persuade them to do so. So let me end by assuring them on my honour that the pleasure is really much greater than the pain.

MASTER AND MAN
(1937)

It has lately been announced that the Professional Golfers' Association desire some legislation on the subject of caddies at the Open Championship. What they want, as I gather, is a very definitely fixed fee for carrying, and a rule of first come first served, the player to take his luck and the caddie that comes to him in rotation. The question may be at present regarded as *sub judice*, in so far as that I may possibly be a member of a committee before which it may be brought. Therefore it would not, perhaps, be right for me to express my view on the particular point. It may, however, be permissible to talk more generally on a question which arises, not only in regard to professional players and championships.

In a general way, then, I should, as a good conservative, always be sorry to see anything which should render less close and intimate the relationship between the player and his caddie. When a caddie declares that 'we won,' it is no mere figure of speech; the caddie in such case regards himself, and very often rightly, as an important member of the victorious alliance. This alliance is an ancient, pleasant and picturesque feature of golf which it would be a pity to destroy or weaken without good cause. I seem to remember that, a good many years ago now, the Ladies' Golf Union were agitated because, in their championship, some ladies had their brothers or fathers to carry for them, and some had professionals. This, it was thought, gave those players an unfair advantage.

I am so thoroughly conservative as to ask why they should not have that advantage if they can. It is not everybody who can profit by the wisdom and experience of a good caddie; some of us may do better with just a silent and sober machine. Personally, I rank myself rather in the latter class; but if a player can be nursed and helped by his caddie, good luck to him! It is a part of the tradition of the game which I should be very sorry to see destroyed. Unless my memory has become addled, when Mr Maxwell made his startling début in the Amateur Championship at Muirfield by beating Mr John Ball and Mr Hilton, he had Ben Sayers carrying for him. It is impossible to say how much of a help it was to him to have so stalwart a henchman, so astute an adviser, at his elbow. For all I know, some people would call that 'unfair'; but I like to think of it. At that same Muirfield, when Harry Vardon won his first championship he had his brother Tom carrying for him in playing off the tie against Taylor. Here was surely a pleasant and proper confederacy. It would have been much duller if Vardon had merely had number something, drawn out of a hat, to carry his clubs to victory.

Whatever the occasion, I feel a good deal of sympathy with any golfer who cannot get his own particular caddie if he wants him. I also feel sympathy with the caddie who cannot get his regular employer, to whose interests he is often devoted. Some caddies are a great deal better than others; they are artists in their way, as compared with mere labouring hinds; and it is a little hard if they are to be treated as such unskilled labourers, no better and no worse than their fellows. It is still harder if they have to carry, not for some considerable player, but for some cumberer of the ground, and lose all chance of the possibly substantial fruits of victory. There never was an employer so rigidly conscientious that he did not give his caddie a modest reward, if he won even a monthly medal, and it is inhuman to expect him not to. Something in the nature of a fixed price for caddies is a great blessing to players. We have all suffered from not knowing at times how much we ought to pay, and have subsequently wanted to kick ourselves for our weakness in having paid too much; but the best principles can be carried too far, and, even for the sake of those advantages, I do not like the notion of master and man being separated because the master has not arrived at the caddie-master's box at exactly the propitious moment. Neither, for that manner, am I in love with trade union principles if we can get along without them; and there seems to me, who am admittedly no political economist, something in this proposal which tends in that direction.

In any argument on this subject there will, as a rule, be found ranged against one another two schools of thought. One school says that it does not care a straw what sort of caddie it has; the other declares that it has often been made—if occasionally also marred—by its caddie. It is largely, no doubt, a matter of individual temperament. For myself, I have often been able to recognise the resplendent virtues of a caddie, so long as he does not carry for me. That is because, as I am perfectly conscious, I am not very good at being advised, and I thoroughly dislike being ordered about. There are many caddies who know all there is to be known about their business, and are wholly admirable with the right kind of golfer; but I am, for them, the wrong kind, and they would fret me into a madhouse. On the other hand, I have known an almost inarticulate caddie whose sympathy, felt

though unheard, was a prop and stay. A—to me—
excellent caddie was a negro boy who carried my clubs in the
Walker Cup match on the National Golf Links. He knew his
job, but we hardly exchanged a word until we came to the
thirty-fifth hole. At this point, being dormy two and on the
green in two, whereas my adversary was in a bunker, I
turned to that caddie and said, from the very bottom of an
agitated heart: 'I believe I'm going to win,' and a shining
smile of angelic sweetness spread from ear to ear across his
sable countenance.

Small boys can be the very best of caddies, even though
their minds stray a little, sometimes, from the matter in
hand. Even that is not necessarily fatal, for I never had a
better caddie than a boy picked up in the streets of Gullane,
who was overcome with an artist's joy at the beauty of
Archerfield and made expeditions into the rough to find and
show me baby peewits. That was, however, in the intervals,
and he was so keen that once, when my partner and I won a
foursome on the home green at Luffness, he broke into a
subdued clapping. Boys, as Sir Walter Simpson said, are
more 'scoldable' than men; and yet it is hard to scold them
for that which is sometimes their failing, a cheerful and
persistent loquacity. They are apt to tell us long stories
about the deeds of some local hero, and also to draw
exceedingly wounding comparisons between his prowess
and our own. And, *à propos*, Dr Tweddell told me an
agreeable story the other day of the caddie who carried for
him the first time he ever played at St Andrews. He was
playing first, I think, for Aberdeen University against St
Andrews University, and Mr D. H. Kyle was his opponent.
After two good tee shots to the first hole, Mr Kyle had just to
play the odd and put his ball on the green with an iron club.
On Dr Tweddell asking which iron he should take, he was

met with the advice to take a brassie and hit as hard as he could, since he would not reach the burn. 'But,' mildly protested Dr Tweddell, 'Mr Kyle got over with an iron.' 'Ah,' answered the caddie, 'but he's a grand player.'

THE WILL TO WIN
(1938)

If an article at the very beginning of a new year is tradition-
ally retrospective, one which comes with the end of the first
week in the year must surely look forward to the future, and
that in the most encouraging possible manner. I am writing
the article in advance because I hope, at the beginning of
January, to be having a little golfing holiday by the sea, and
that is encouraging for me, but can hardly rouse enthusiasm
in the breasts of others. There is likewise the fact that for the
first time for several weeks my lawn has been green instead
of white, and for the first time for still more weeks I have hit
some shots on a golf course of almost incredible muddiness;
but that, too, is a selfish reason for cheerfulness.

It is less selfish to point out that this eighth day of January
will, if the weather behaves itself, see the tournament for the
President's Putter in full swing at Rye. That, I hope, may
encourage the selectors for the Walker Cup, because never
has there been so strong a field for this tournament, and it
contains several possibles and probables for the match in
June; may they all play brilliantly! Still, most of us are not
selectors and are not going to be selected; we are reasonably
and properly patriotic, but we want to be encouraged primarily about our own little shots and our own little games.
While I was vainly searching for the right and cheerful topic

the post brought me a letter from a correspondent, and in it was the right text. Of course, I have lost his letter, because I lose everything, but his words are graven on my memory.

He told me that he had been playing a four-ball match with three more or less venerable companions of whom the eldest was seventy-five years old. They came to the last short hole in the round, and on the teeing ground some doubtless divine prompting caused him to ask the old gentleman, if I may so term him, if he had ever done a hole in one. 'No,' was the gallant answer, 'I never have, but I shall now,' and thereupon he lifted up his club and smote the ball into the hole. The story goes on that the hero treated the party to champagne for luncheon, but resolutely refused to provide a bottle of whisky for his caddie. To him he gave a pair of sound boots and also some warm clothes for his children. This was in both respects an admirable example, but it has led me away from the central incident.

We often whip ourselves into an artificial courage by saying of a more or less long putt: 'I'm going to hole this one,' and on very, very rare occasions we succeed. I have even heard people facetiously observe that they mean to hole a tee shot, but I have certainly seen them succeed. And the feat—I will not say fluke—is the more remarkable, the will to victory more glorious, at seventy-five than at an earlier age. 'Twenty-seven is not very old,' as is said in *Bab Ballads*. Similarly, seventy-five is not very young. The vista of future short holes is not at that age limitless, and, moreover, there are not so many short holes in a round as there used to be, because some of them grow out of reach. Only the other day a distinguished architect, talking ecstatically of a new short hole he had designed, told me that it would be chiefly of interest to those who could carry 220 yards, whereupon my own interest in it seemed partially to fade away. At seventy-five there are a good many holes that lose interest in this way, and yet this intrepid old party said he was going to hole his tee shot, and he did. 'He must be a first-rater,' said Sam. 'A1,' replied Mr Roker.

The nearest approach to this splendid story is one to be found in Mr Hilton's golfing reminiscences. It concerned almost his earliest tournament, in which, incidentally, his frequent opponent in after years, Freddie Tait, also took part. It was at North Berwick, and in one match Mr Arthur Molesworth of Westward Ho! met a local hero by name, if I remember rightly, Forrest. The formidable Forrest was dormy one and on the home green, not far from the hole, in two, while Mr Molesworth, having met misfortune, was still off the green in three. Quite undaunted by this apparently hopeless situation, he walked up and down, up and down, studying the line of his run-up, until some of the crowd grew restive and made opprobrious comments. He turned to the loudest of them and said: 'You think I'm not going to hole this. You'll see!' and thereupon he did hole it. His opponent, not unnaturally horrified, took three putts 'from nowhere,' and lost the match at the nineteenth. Most of us, feeble folk as we are, should not dare to say such a thing, and, if we said it a hundred times, the chance would never 'come off.' To be able to say it once and then bring it off surely bespeaks some greatness of soul.

If we ever did say such a thing we should say it without conviction, and that is fatal. The will to victory is not of much avail without the belief in victory, and it is very hard to entertain that belief at, let us say, three down with four to play. A few years ago there was a cheerful and flamboyant young man in the Oxford side who was asked in the University match how he was getting on. He replied, so the story goes: 'I'm two down, but I'm sure to win. He's cracking.' Whether 'he' did crack I do not know, but at any rate that valiant flaunter of the malicious fates did win. Most of us, if we ever ventured on any such remark, would add 'Touching wood' or 'In a good hour be it spoken,' and then all the virtue goes out of our noble bombast. Even when we are four up we are almost afraid of admitting it, lest some Nemesis pursue our boasting. We like to think that it is lest our adversary's feelings be hurt, if he hears us, but that is a pretence. It is cold fear that is at the bottom of our good manners.

Harry Vardon used to say that whatever the situation there was only one thing to do, namely, to 'go on hitting the ball.' That is, no doubt, a great truth, and to make this resolution internally—we can hardly proclaim it aloud —can save us from collapse. It is probably better than a more obviously magnificent resolution, much less likely to be fulfilled. One of the difficulties of resolutions, as it seems to me, is that they have the effect of stringing us up, of making us rigid, when our hope lies in being relaxed. It is a very good resolution to keep the eye on the ball; yet we often see someone, who has been told that he is looking up, so tautening and tightening himself in the tremendousness of his determination that the head springs up faster than ever.

I have never forgotten that once, when I was in this parlous state, a wise man cured me by telling me deliberately to let my head turn a little; the effect was, for the time being, magical. Some resolutions can make us try too hard. I doubt, for instance, whether a concentrated ferocity of determin-ation to hole every long putt is of much use. On the other hand, a modest vow to be up with every long putt may at least stop us from being short every time. I am assuming, of course, that we are not splendid old gentlemen of seventy-five. Ordinary rules do not apply to them. They are in the heroes' class.

THE RABBIT'S IDEAL
(1939)

Not long ago my neighbour at dinner urged on me the duty of writing an article on the ideal course for rabbits. Under the mellowing influence of the dinner—it was a very good one—this seemed to me a capital subject. I did point out to him some of the difficulties, but I promised to see what could be done about it. Now that I sit down to redeem my promise, the difficulties seem so many and so overwhelming that I hesitate. However, my word has been given, and so here goes.

The initial difficulty of defining a rabbit may be lightly treated. I suppose that he is roughly a golfer with a handicap well advanced in the 'teens. The real trouble is that two rabbits of the same handicap may posses utterly different tastes and ambitions. For instance, I once stayed at Pine Valley, near Philadelphia, which has the reputation of being the hardest course in the world. Possibly it is not quite so terrible as it seems on a first acquaintance, but there is no doubt that appalling things may there befall one, in the shape of lakes and firwoods and heather, to say nothing of bunkers. I asked my partner what the more elderly and stout and incompetent among the members thought of it and whether they did not grow weary of so hectic and prostrating a struggle. He answered that they most certainly did not and that if, having never before beaten 125, they suddenly went round in 119, they were 'tickled to death.'

I could only conclude that the American rabbit was, on the whole, a braver and more glorious creature than is our home-bred animal. I cannot believe that the average British rabbit would regard Pine Valley, great course that it is, as his ideal. That is one side of the picture, and now here is another. My friend of the dinner cited St George's, Sandwich, as a course that he found altogether too tremendous for him. He gave the sixteenth hole as an example. I answered, rather surprised, that no doubt a good straight shot was wanted to reach the green, but still— 'Look at that bunker on the right of the green,' he cut in. 'It is as deep as the pit.' I am still surprised at his instance, because there are at Sandwich bunkers and hazards, as I should have thought, far more formidable, and a short and erratic hitter may have a very bad time in them, so that he may very likely say that he would prefer to play somewhere else. Yet there is this to be said on the other side, that if the rabbit can suffer greatly among mighty hills and in mighty bunkers, he can also enjoy greatly getting over them. The good player thinks nothing of it, but the rabbit who has surmounted a famous hazard can be made happy for the day. Surely his modest joys would be diminished if he were never afraid and never triumphed over his fears.

I must in all honesty bring forward any evidence against me that I know of, and so I may quote a golfer with whom I once travelled in a very slow four-wheeler from a golf course to a station. He suddenly joined in a discussion with the words: 'I have lately been playing on the ideal golf course. It has no hazards of any description.' It was a startling and splendid remark, but I am not sure that he was quite serious; I think he was delicately poking fun at us who were arguing too solemnly; I do not believe that he was a rabbit at all. Whether he was serious or not, I have sometimes shared his views.

There is a course of my acquaintance, set on noble downs, which used once almost to answer his description. Today there is rough grass on either hand and one must drive tolerably straight, but in elder days there was a wood and a road and one or two major hazards, but apart from these there was a vast expanse of untroubled turf and one could drive where one pleased. Never was there such a perfect golfing rest cure, and, because there was no need to do so, one always drove as straight as a line. Too much of it might have become enervating, but a little of it was gorgeous fun, and I suppose my friend of the dinner would have deemed it eternal fun.

One thing I take to be tolerably sure, that the ideal course for rabbits must not be too long. He is not, as a rule, very skilful with his brassie, and especially in winter he has a great deal of work to do with his wooden club through the green. It is hard to be precise as to yards, because turf varies in pace, but he will probably be happiest on a course of not more than 6,000 yards or so in length. And yet, having written, I begin to doubt. If he does not want too long a course, why does he so often persist in driving from the back tees when there are the shorter ones staring at him, beckoning him to enjoy himself? I cannot answer that question, and so shall pass on. He will unquestionably be happiest if his good shots are not cruelly used, and he has a right to demand this happiness. He ought always to have a way of safety, narrow, perhaps, but not impossibly so, no matter how mild are his carrying powers. At the same time, unless I misjudge him, he does like to have some lions in his path, in order that he may taste the exquisite joys of escape.

What he likes—I daresay we all like it—is a bunker of horrible aspect into which there is comparatively small chance of getting. This is an amiable weakness which some golfing architects have appreciated to the full. I can think of several courses constructed, to some extent, on this principle. The bunkers are fearful to look at, but difficult to get into, so that we first trifle with our fears and then think ourselves very fine golfers. Of course, the architect is a cunning fellow and does not make his device too obvious, or the effect would be ruined.

As to the greens in this paradise, the rabbit naturally likes to think that he can make his iron shots stop in a professional manner. Therefore he must not have too many greens that run away from him, and he ought to have several where a kindly upward slope at the back enables him to play boldly and without fear of running over. Yet here again cunning is necessary, for too palpable a rampart at the back of a green will disgust anyone. Most certainly he should have at least one green in a crater, where the ball runs round and round perchance to lie beautifully dead at last. He thinks that very good fun, and so, for once in a while, it is. This would be a drab world if there were no greens in hollows to make us believe we have been clever, though we know in our hearts that we have not.

Where the ideal rabbits' course may be I do not know, but among famous courses I believe the nearest approach to it is that greatest of all, St Andrews. It is not too exhaustingly long, at least when the ground is hard and full of running, as it often is. It demands no carrying power from the tee, so that there is no hole where a short shot cannot be safe. It offers, on the whole, plenty of room, and there is no view in the whole world so encouraging to the agitated starter as that vast unbunkered plain between the clubhouse and the burn.

The bunkers have historic names and—perhaps this is a defect from the ideal point of view—some of them are far from easy to get out of; but they hardly ever bar the way inevitably and hopelessly, and are in many cases more likely to trap the tiger than the reasonably unambitious rabbit. The greens are large and not closely hemmed in with trouble, so that it appears—this is sometimes a deceitful appearance—that we have a good margin of error in our approaches. My friend of the dinner has never been there, and I strongly urge him to go. I hope and believe he will enjoy himself; only, if he gets into the Hill bunker, which is rather deep, don't let him blame me!

A HOLLOW FEELING
(1940)

I walked the other day to see some bomb holes—they were hardly worthy the name of craters—which had been made in a piece of open, quiet country near to where I was staying. No amount of hooking or slicing, not the most outrageous over- or under-clubbing, could have accounted for them. There was once a famous summing-up by a famous judge which began, 'The prisoner says he aimed at nothing. Unfortunately he missed it.' It would be entirely applicable to the German who made those holes except that he did not miss nothing; fortunately he hit it with great accuracy. He had rattled my windows for me the night before, and so I felt bound to go and see his holes, but they were hardly worth it save for one. This was in a meadow of sandy soil, so that the hole instantly and pleasantly reminded my golf-warped mind of a pot-bunker: and very deep, but with a little rampart thrown up on one side to prevent getting out being altogether too easy.

I remembered during the last war to have played a round of golf on a Greek course, the name of which has gone from me. The one fact I am sure of is that the only bunkers—or, more strictly, hazards—were shell holes. Recalling that course and now seeing this wasted pot-bunker, I wondered if many golf courses, some of them perhaps old and familiar friends, had had many new bunkers of this kind made in them; further, whether, as is sometimes the case, the accidental bunker had turned out better than any that the architect could devise. If there are any such, I cannot help hoping that some at least will be kept, after the war is over, as memorials and, if they are in rather 'unfair' places so much the better. I know one course, and a very engaging one, at Ormskirk where one had to play sometimes out of Cromwell's trenches, dug during his siege of Lathom House. If that still feels romantic, so may these pot-bunkers to the golfers of nearly three hundred years hence.

What I hope for still more, however—and now my cloven foot is going to appear—is for a new putting green or two made in these bomb craters. I know such greens are now unfashionable and condemned by all the best people; that these are fluky and, if there are too many of them, tiresome; but I maintain that just a very occasional one is fascinating fun. A few months ago on Banstead Downs I saw a green at the bottom of an old gravel pit, overgrown with grass long since, and it gave me a nostalgic and wistful feeling in my inside. I recalled all manner of dear, departed greens in hollows. There was first of all the second green on the old nine-hole course at Felixstowe. It was a one-shot hole, with its teeing-ground close to Willie Fernie's shop, the Martello tower on the right, and a moderately innocuous cross-bunker in the way.

When I call it a one-shot hole I mean for grown-ups. For me, at the age of eight or nine, it demanded a full drive which might carry the bunker, and then a good long pitch, *but* I did it more than once in three, and that was the beauty of the crater; it was so small that, once it had entered, the ball was more likely to lie dead than not. Then there were the fifteenth and seventeenth at Aberdovey, of which the seventeenth is long since dead and is indeed a wild moraine of slate. The fifteenth was always called 'The Crater' and is so still by a few survivors, such as myself, of a vanished epoch. The green is still in the same place, and here and there some traces remain of the old, kindly banks that turned the ball inward to the hole; but where are 'the pineapples,' those elaborately built battlements of bent grass which once grew on the bank in front of the green and were hacked to pieces by niblick shots? That bank has gone altogether. The hole is now, I believe candidly, one of the very finest two-shot holes on any course anywhere for anybody; but, while I admire the new, I loved the old.

The race is not altogether extinct. There is a capital specimen on the new course at Walton Heath—I think the fifteenth. Then—unless, as Mr Peggotty said, my wits have gone birds'-nesting—the sixth green at St Anne's is in a distinct crater, and so is the third at Burnham. They are not as friendly and helpful as some of those I have mentioned, but I still have pleasant recollections of a very bad shot of mine at Burnham ending very close to the hole.

No doubt there are others that I ought to recall, but it is the ghosts that haunt me. There was that one at Formby which marked the leaving of the flatter country and the setting out into the noble land of mountains and mountain gorges. Admittedly, the short hole, with its green almost overlooking the old crater, is incomparably better, and yet sentiment may drop its tear. So it may over the old sixth (I think it was) at Hunstanton. There, too, a far better—indeed a horribly good and narrow—green has been planted, looking down contemptuously on the poor old hollow.

Lastly, there was the seventeenth at Sandwich, which had in the highest degree all the good—or bad—qualities of a crater, since, after two strokes that appeared much of a muchness, one ball would be found to have shot away across the green and the other would be nestling by the flag. At such a critical moment in the round it required either a stolid calm or very well disciplined behaviour to prevent oneself from running to the top of the hill to see what had happened. I was all square going to that hole in my first University match, and I am very sure that I ran. Cricket is not the only game that can boast of its 'glorious uncertainty,' but that of golf is not quite what it was since craters were abandoned.

ABSIT OMEN
(1941)

Golfers will do anything in reason to avert the evil chance. If we meet a friend, whom we suspect of doing well, in the course of a medal round and are so indiscreet or so inhuman as to ask his score, it is ten to one that he will answer us with vague generalities and conjectures that he is sure to come to grief before he has done. Similarly, no one who is playing a match in a tournament willingly says that he is three up; the most that he will admit is that he is 'doing pretty well at present.' Nor is this said from any desire to spare his adversary's feelings; it springs wholly from a fear of provoking some terrible Nemesis. These phenomena are indeed so well known that I should be almost ashamed to mention them again did they not lead up to a rather different and singular instance of 'touch-woodishness,' if I may so term it.

I have just received a long and pleasant letter from a young friend of mine, a very good golfer, who, having been till lately playing in Trinidad, is now, when he gets the chance, struggling with the sand greens of Nigeria. He, too, wants to avert the evil chance, but it is, as will be seen, an altruistic desire. He has developed a habit of doing holes in one, and as sure as ever he does it some frightful public catastrophe ensues. The first time was in the meeting at

Westward Ho! before he went abroad. That was on September 1, 1939. He had never achieved the feat before, but his pleasure was short-lived; a passing caddie told him that the Germans had invaded Poland. In the following year he was playing on a short course in Trinidad, and again holed his tee shot. It was the very day that the German hordes poured into Holland and Belgium. So now he is frightened of playing golf lest the malignancy of Fate should not yet have worked itself out and a third one should produce something still worse.

I have endeavoured to exorcise these fears by telling him that the third time is lucky, and further that I did a hole in one during the last war, in Macedonia, without producing any visible effect on the campaign one way or the other. It was a beautiful hole (I laid it out myself), and it was in a way unique. It was played twice in the round from diametrically opposite tees, and was at once the first hole and the last of the round. A better natural green I never saw, for it consisted of a small hollow, very shallow, set on a low hill-top, with the ground falling away on every side. The first hole was comparatively simple, since only a mashie-niblick pitch was needed and there was nothing worse than broken ground in the way. The last, as was only proper, was more testing; the tee shot was considerably longer, and the bank guarding the green steeper, while between tee and green stretched an oozy and ominous piece of marsh. It was a lovely green, with one engaging little tree casting a patch of starveling shade upon its verge, and I have never either forgotten or forgiven the RE's who, in the watches of the night, cut down the tree and stripped off the turf for their own base purposes. My only consolation was and is that no one else could ever again do it in one.

When, by the way, I did it, it was at the last hole and not

the first, so that there was no fear of any personal golfing disaster overwhelming me. Fate could not harm me; the round was ended, and that, for most ordinarily excitable people, is a not unimportant point. These flukes in the grand manner are apt to have a disturbing effect, and therefore it is well that they should come as late in the round as possible. If they happen early, we are rather light-headed for a hole or two afterwards, and before we settle down again Fate will take its chance.

Not many courses have a last hole that can be done in one, but a notable exception is Prestwick, where the last green is within reach of a modern full shot; the books set it down as 283 yards long. I remember that on one occasion in the Army Championship a gallant officer holed his tee shot there, and that must have been a thoroughly dramatic occasion, with the seats outside the clubhouse filled with spectators. However, as he had taken, if I remember rightly, ten to the first hole, perhaps his transports were modified. There was a very famous one done at Prestwick at the seventeenth in the days of the old twelve-hole course. That was in the Open Championship, by Jamie Anderson in his last round; so he had not much time in which to lose his head. In any case he had given sufficient proofs of imperturbability, for at the fifteenth he had holed a full iron shot and at the sixteenth a very long putt. I have always felt sorry for the man who was second in that Championship; I think he had very good cause to complain of destiny, for after that series of outrages Jamie Anderson won by one single shot.

We should be better golfers than we are if we could overcome the feeling that the Fates, after favouring us grossly, are sure to turn against us. It is much too strong for most of us. To hole one or two good putts is eminently encouraging, for we think, truly enough, that we are hitting the ball well and we have confidence in our latest new method, whatever may be. But when the putts are too long or too frequent, then we grow afraid and make perhaps the most lethal of remarks, that we must have had our ration. I have heard something like it said by one of the calmest and sanest, as he is one of the best, of golfers, Mr Francis Ouimet. It was in the Amateur Championship at Deal in 1923. In the morning he had to play one very fine player—I think it was Mr Tolley, but I am away from books. At any rate, the putts went in from everywhere and Mr Ouimet won easily. In the afternoon it was the semi-final and he met Mr Wethered. Now the ball obstinately refused to go in and he was more or less easily beaten, and said afterwards that he could not get away from feeling that he had had his full day's allowance in the morning.

One of the wonderful things, as I remember it, of the late Mr W. J. Travis's win at Sandwich in 1904 was that he holed some really long putts in every round, certainly in every round after he had begun to attract attention and the American terror had spread across the links. If he ever allowed himself to think that he had had his ration, he showed no signs of it. Indeed, the vision, as I recall it, of that slight, serious figure, black cigar in mouth, watching the ball as it ran towards the hole, rather conveyed that he expected it to drop every time. He was not only a superb putter, but he had a new club, the Schenectade, and faith in a new putter can sometimes endure for a considerable spell. I rather hope my young friend in Nigeria will not buy a new iron. If he does he is sure to hole another tee shot with catastrophic results.

THE GOLFLESS HOLIDAY
(1942)

Last week I took as my text a letter from one friend whom the course of his military duties had taken to the neighbourhood of a pleasant links. Whereupon, aided by two 74s, he had been once more filled with enthusiasm for the game. This week I have had a letter from another which is clearly intended by Providence to supply me with a corollary. This friend—a very old one—is just about to take a well-earned holiday. He is clearly the bravest and most resolute of men. He may be the wisest as well, or he may be the most foolish. As to that I cannot make up my mind, and the reader must judge. He is going to the greatest of all links, and he is taking no golf clubs with him, but only a shooting-stick. 'I intend,' he writes, 'to spend a week there in laughing at the golfing foibles of my friends,' and he adds firmly: 'I am sure I am right.'

He does not attempt to propitiate me by any excuses, but he does give an explanation. He has not hit a single ball for a whole year; he has neither time nor inclination for intensive practice beforehand, and he does not feel 'in the mood.' If he took his bag of clubs with him—and it is a large one, for he was a great patron of the clubmakers—he would only bring it back again, 'disillusioned and profoundly unhappy'; and so he is leaving it behind. I shall admit one thing, that he is a man of character. I, too, have been to that noble spot without my clubs and been very happy there, but then there was a championship that I had to watch. To go there for a holiday without clubs demands a captaincy of the soul to which I can make no pretensions. Am I not right in saying that it shows either great wisdom or great folly?

Not being in the mood for golf is a horribly common complaint in such times as these: I am suffering from it myself at the present moment, but shall I not be convalescent—touching wood—towards the end of September when the time comes for me to look up, quite superfluously, in *Bradshaw* the same dear old train? The appetite comes in eating, a proverb of which my old friend may find out the truth before his week is sped. Meanwhile, I like to picture him after a late and lazy breakfast strolling down to the clubhouse on his first morning. He will exchange cheerful, almost uproarious, greetings with those who appear to have been sitting in exactly the same chairs ever since he was last there. He will then ensconce himself behind the big window, drinking in great draughts of felicity as he contemplates the familiar scene. Ever and anon he will indulge in a biting quip or two as to the eccentricities of those driving off from the first teeing ground. Here, he will say to himself, is the perfectly restful holiday alike for body and mind, and he will be more than ever complacent about his resolution.

Presently there will appear on the tee four friends whom it would particularly amuse him to watch, and with an effort he will dislodge himself from his window seat and, shouldering his shooting-stick in a jaunty manner, will set out with them. If they make bad shots he will guffaw; if they make good ones he will cordially and unenviously admire; if they are kept back by those tiresome people in front he will be no whit impatient, but will repose placidly on the shooting-stick. He may even 'remember with advantages' how once upon a time, when haply I was playing with him, we were delayed in an intolerable manner by the Bishop of Barchester and his three octogenarian companions and took three and a half hours, full measure, to get round. In short, that first morning and even perhaps the whole first two days will be sheer bliss.

About the third day he may, as I calculate, become a little less sure that he was right. Exactly how the blow will fall I cannot say. No doubt he will borrow somebody's putter on one green or another, but this will hardly do it, for putting is so separate and self-contained a branch of golf that a little indulgence will not inspire a wild lust for a whole round. Rather I imagine that one of the four he is watching will insidiously put into his hand a most seductive iron, or perhaps a spoon, together with a couple of balls, and suggest that he have a smack or two on the New Course next door and then rejoin the party later on. That will be the crucial moment. If he hits a good smack he will long to play a round, and if he does not he may lack the fortitude required to leave off with a bad one. In either case he will feel bitterly sorry that he did not bring his own clubs with him. He will be like the man in the story who died and found himself on the most beautiful golf course with rows of shining clubs ready to his hand. He thought that some fortunate mistake had been made by the recording angel and that he must be in Heaven after all, when another damned soul enlightened him by saying: 'There are no balls.'

This mood of not being in the mood is a very sensitive and mutable thing; it does not take much to overset it. The man who thinks he has given up golf for a while is like to him who thinks he has given up smoking. The abstainer from tobacco is so sure that he has overcome the craving that, out of pure bravado and in order to prove he is right, he accepts a cigarette. It tastes like nothing in particular, and he is still more sure he is right, but somehow he takes another and then he is done for. So the golfing abstainer's first shot with the borrowed iron may not feel very good; it will probably be mistimed and jar his fingers, but the second or third ball will fly sweetly away and it will be all over with him.

A very little thing will bring back the lost mood. The other day a friend at a club told me casually that he had been having a day at Hoylake. That might have left me tranquil, even indifferent, but he described with a positively infernal eloquence how it had been blowing hard (don't I know that wind?), how he had just got past the corner of the field with his first tee shot and then, with the very best brassie shot he could hit into the teeth of the wind, had reached the edge of the green and obtained his four. I gathered that after this he was less successful, but I scarcely heard him, for I was lost in a selfish dream of Hoylake. I knew I could not get up at that first hole in two against the wind (I wonder, incidentally, whether the tee was at all forward), but I reckoned at what holes that same wind would help me. It would make the tee shot to the Telegraph comparatively simple; it would blow me kindly along at the Dun, and surely the cross-bunker at the home hole would not catch my second. Instantly I felt in the mood to take the next train to Liverpool and imagined with what a thrill I should look down on a sulphurous Widnes out of my carriage window.

I remember how, a good many years ago, I arrived at a familiar and hospitable house and, after the first greetings with half a dozen fellow-guests, I exclaimed: 'Well, whom do I have to play tomorrow?' The answer came in chorus: 'Oh, we none of us play golf.' It was too true, for every single one of them had something the matter with one limb or another. How sorry I then felt for them! Sorrier, perhaps, than I should now when I understand more of these inevitable afflictions. Nevertheless, if, all being well, I go there soon I shall take my bag, a light one with half a dozen clubs in it, and though I am sure, in my friend's words, to be disillusioned, I hope I shall not be too profoundly unhappy. Meanwhile, I unreservedly withdraw any malign remarks I may have made about him. I trust and believe that he will enjoy his holiday.

HORSES FOR COURSES
(1943)

It is interesting to know how the war affects the life of other people in its golfing aspects as in far more serious ones. So I was glad to receive lately from a kind correspondent a cutting from *The New York Sun* of March 1. Here is a photograph of a number of middle-aged gentlemen, one of them in uniform and all well wrapped up, sitting in a brake of more or less venerable appearance: it is drawn by two white horses, having something of the proud and dignified look of the 'liberty horses' of the circus. These are the members of the Oakland Golf Club, now deprived of petrol and resuming their ancient manner of getting to their course. The brake was made in 1905 and was obtained from an estate in Connecticut, while the horses came all the way from Iowa. 'Dressed in a brass-buttoned coachman's coat and derby,' says my cutting, 'brandishing an old-fashioned whip, Jack Dowling, who said all his life had been spent with horses, drove his first load of Oakland members to the club from the Long Island Bayside Station yesterday in an antiquated but well-preserved Brewster Brake. The distance of one and three-tenths miles was covered in fourteen minutes flat.'

I did not play at Oakland when I was in the United States with the Walker Cup team of 1922. Most of the rest of us spent a day there, but I had some engagement in New York and could not go. I have always been sorry and those who went enjoyed themselves very much and said that the club had a particularly engaging and friendly atmosphere of its own. How they travelled there I cannot now remember; presumably it was by car, but the golfers of today seem comparatively fortunate in having less than a mile and a half to travel from the station. Cars are sadly spoiling things and many of us used to travel a good deal farther than that, and behind horses much less impressive than these noble steeds from Iowa, in order to get to our golf, and, not having known better days, did not think ourselves very hardly used.

My mind has gone ranging back into the past over the various methods of transport to the course before the era of cars. There was, first of all, 'Shanks's mare.' Those who know Aberdovey (I apologise for mentioning it yet again) may admire the heroism of its pioneers when I tell them that in prehistoric ages we tramped all the way to the railway crossing, hard by the present Cader tee, and then on again till a point beyond the fifteenth green of today. Then at long last we started to play to what is now the fifth hole. The trudge home again for lunch seems in retrospect to have been rather exhausting and yet we would play our two rounds a day.

There were not even bicycles to help us and, though our legs may have ached the more, we may have played the better, for to my mind a bicycle is a most treacherous ally. To be sure, it gets one over the ground, but after a certain not very long distance it produces some odd and disconcerting effect on the wrists, whereby the player plunges the club-head deep into the ground or scalps the extreme top of the ball and generally does not know whether he is on his head or his heels. Such at least used to be my doleful experience, after bicycling from near Machynlleth to Aberdovey or from

Cambridge to Royston. The distance in each case was not great, eleven or twelve miles or so, nor did one feel a penny the worse for it until one tried to hit the ball; then how varied and desperate were the effects!

It has, of course, often been told how when A. J. T. Allan won the Amateur Championship at Muirfield in 1897, he daily came down by train from Edinburgh and then bicycled from Drem Station to the links. I am not sure how far Drem is from Gullane, but it is a perceptible number of miles. Perhaps it was just within a safe radius or perhaps Allan, a singularly calm and imperturbable person, did not suffer from my disease in that respect. Incidentally, my American cutting tells how the famous Walter Travis used regularly to bicycle from his home at Flushing to Oakland, but then again I do not know the distance.

At Cambridge I used often to bicycle down to the course at Coldham Common, but that distance was short enough to be harmless. If, however, one felt opulent and reckless and had a partner of like mind, one took a hansom, and I have almost as tender memories of jingling down the Newmarket Road and through the purlieus of Barnwell as of a hansom in the dip in Piccadilly, a Piccadilly of cheerful twinkling lights and not of stygian darkness. One truly remarkable instance of enthusiasm blended with patience returns from those Cambridge times. It was on some day when there were few if any trains—it may have been Christmas Day—and several of us jogged slowly all the way to Royston and back again in some closed and hearse-like vehicle. Nor was this purely the result of youthful effervescence; I was young enough indeed, but the rest of the party consisted of middle-aged fellows of colleges. 'Pray how did you manage to do it?' may ask the pampered golfer of but yesterday, and I am bound to say that I stand amazed at the recollection. No doubt it was

worth it, just as it was a hundred times worth it to travel by
the slowest of all slow trains to Mildenhall and then walk
back half a mile along the railway line and then climb a fence
and then jump over a wet ditch to the fourth green. The walk
back after tea in the dark of a winter's evening had a spice of
excitement, for the train would come along behind us in a
stealthy manner and one must leap for life off the track.

That pleasant old word 'brake' must bring back sentimental memories to all who recall Woking *consule Planco*.
After starting early from Waterloo (how slippery was the
granite pavement on Waterloo Bridge to nailed shoes!) and
stopping at Surbiton, Walton, Weybridge, Byfleet and
heaven knows where besides, we alighted at Woking station
and made an undignified competitive rush down the platform to get a place in the brake. If one missed the brake, one
took an ancient fly, which went perceptibly slower, and by
the time the course was reached, after a final walk over wet
heather, all the brakesmen had their golf balls placed in a
serried line on the first tee.

There is undoubtedly one thing to be said for the motor-
car that it does not dump all the golfers on the course at the
same moment; but there was also something to be said for
the brake. That laborious journey in three or four stages was
very friendly and companionable and led to the making of
games against the following Sunday. The fact that one
would hesitate to endure it now does not prove that it was
not agreeable then. The poet's well-known remarks about
'sorrow's crown of sorrow' had no application.

I do not know what is the technical difference if any—
perhaps the dictionary could tell me—between a cab and a
fly. A cab seems to me to signify primarily a closed vehicle, a
four-wheeler with straw at the bottom. A fly is essentially
a country vehicle such as may still sometimes be found at

rustic stations, and it is open; perhaps an ancient victoria, which in its best days has been a carriage. However that may be, it is flies which memory connects with those old journeys to golf courses, journeys along roads sometimes white with summer dust. It was in a fly some forty or more years ago that three others and I drove from Edinburgh to Barnton on a Sunday, with our clubs securely hidden under horse rugs, lest the sight of them should give offence

I had almost forgotten one means of transport, that by water. Today the Dublin golfer goes by car all the way to the lovely links of Portmarnock, but once upon a time the final stage was made, if I am right, in a sailing boat. It was not a very long one, and yet I seem to remember one return journey in strong wind and a snowstorm, when I was privately glad that it was no longer. There was, too, a very brief journey by ferry to Littlehampton, a fitting prelude to a lobster lunch of scrumptious quality. Yet another pleasant but very dim memory is that of getting to Bembridge by boat and of John Low addressing the boatman in a cheerful manner with, 'Now you licensed brigand!' A year or two ago one could still get some petrol by filling up tremendous forms alleging, among other things, that there were no alternative means of transport. Well, I have enjoyed thinking over the alternative means by which we were once upon a time transported to our game and must ask forgiveness for much garrulity inspired by the picture of those Oakland golfers.

FOSSILS OF THE PAST
(1944)

One of the Sherlock Holmes stories—*The Adventure of the Blue Carbuncle* unless I am mistaken—begins with Holmes studying an ancient hat which has accidentally come into his possession, and deducing from it that the owner has considerable intellectual development and that his wife has ceased to love him. I feel a little like Holmes at this moment as, without his intellectual development, I sit poring over three old clubs, one wooden and two iron, the latter long since encrusted with red rust. They live in the house which has lately given me kindly refuge, and have lived there so long that their story is 'lost evermo''; nobody knows who bought them or whence they came. They are not really so very old, since the brassie is of the socket and not the 'skeered' variety, a fact which gives some clue, and one of the iron clubs is unquestionably a mashie and there was a time—I remember it myself—when mashies did not exist. Nevertheless, in their present derelict condition they seem to belong to a prehistoric age.

As to the brassie, at any rate, Sherlockian gifts are not needed to deduce that the owner was no judge of a club, since this is, on the whole, the worst club I ever saw. It is at once very light and as stiff as a ramrod; waggle it as you may, there is no vestige of that spring which Old Tom so poetically termed the 'music' in the shaft. The head, which is exceedingly small, not that this is a damning fault in itself, is so put on that the heel projects horribly. It has 'slice' written all over it, and the grip is on a par with the rest of it, for it is of odiously slimy leather which slips out of the hand. It has obviously had plenty of wear, but there are no marks on the face from which any deduction of value can be made. I give it up.

The two iron clubs are more interesting, not perhaps from a detective point of view, but as historical objects. One of them for instance I find decidedly 'intriguing' because it is hard to identify. A modern iron bears its name and number; its exact place in club society is clear for all men to see; but what is this? It is hardly a cleek, for it is too lofted; it is hardly an iron, at any rate, after the fashion of today, for it is too shallow in the face. Perhaps in its youthful prime it was called an 'approaching cleek,' and the happy owner, when he bore it all glittering from the shop, thought he would lay all his run-up shots dead ever afterwards. The mashie is just a mashie, though with a face smaller and less deep than is now the mode. Both have fat leather grips with plenty of black padding underneath, and I think I am justified in deducing that the owner did not use the overlapping grip.

One other tentative deduction I may make from these clubs, namely that the owner had rather a forcing style, since both shafts are bent into a hoop. That old phrase comes naturally back to me, and yet it is a long time since I saw shafts so bent, for those of steel remain as a rule rigidly and unbendingly correct. There used to be something fascinating in such a shaft, especially in a driving iron. The bend rather reduced the loft on the face and conduced to the hitting of a ball that bored its way well through the wind. I remember a certain driving iron of my own which I once stole—well, well, I must not grow sentimentally reminiscent. Enough that there was a certain tortuous charm about such shafts; but it was a day of wrath, a dreadful day, when the shaft at last broke, as break it must. The head developed an incompatibility of temper with the new and straight shaft with which it was mated; it seemed to pine away, missing its old companion, and too often became useless ever afterwards.

All three of these ancient fossils are beyond doubt shockingly bad clubs, and yet I find myself growing rather fond of them when I take them surreptitiously out of the umbrella-stand and waggle them in the front hall; they remind me of certain old clubs of my own. In these days of steel shafts and rustless heads everybody's clubs are both good to feel and comely in aspect, and my own are, I believe, just as good as anybody else's, but in the pre-steel days I was one of those always deemed by their friends to have bad clubs. I liked them but nobody else did and I grew well accustomed to somebody picking one of them up, giving it a contemptuous glance and returning it with the words: 'Well, how the devil you can play with a thing like that I can't imagine.' There was always something definitely ramshackle and disreputable about their appearance. Sometimes I had shortened their shafts in my own amateurish way with some kitchen implement, and if the binding of the grip became loose I would remedy it with a tin-tack. The worthiest of clubs is not likely to look its best after such treatment.

Those, however, were extreme cases, and apart from such rough and ready doctoring my clubs would insist on looking shabby. I recall one in particular which was in my bag and moreover did not undistinguished service on the one occasion when I had the honour of playing in the Walker Cup. It was an aged spoon, which I was using for my shots through the green. There was very little paint left on the head, so that the patches of grey appeared through the yellow; all symptoms of varnish had long departed; the leather of the grip was rapidly disintegrating, and that blessed binding had come loose again so that a piece of string depended and whistled through the air as I swung. Mr Fownes and I had as our referee Mr Ward, a good golfer and in his day a very famous player at baseball. For the first six holes he spoke never a word, but at the seventh, I think it was, I made rather a good shot with my disreputable friend. 'May I look at that club?' said Mr Ward, and having gazed at it for some time he handed it back with the words: 'If anybody were to tell you that club had been played with in an international match you wouldn't believe him.'

It was during that American tour that my clubs became perceptibly more down-at-heel and out-at-elbows, if such terms are applicable to clubs, than ever before. The free-born American caddie neither tees your ball nor cleans your clubs, and all the members of a golf club pay, or in those days did pay, a certain subscription to have them cleaned in the professional's shop. That was an excellent plan for those who played regularly on the same course, but when one was visiting a series of courses one grew a little tired of paying to have one's irons cleaned and then departing before this had been done. So I resolved to let them, so to speak, return to Nature, and in time they attained a fine rich black colour not wholly unbecoming. But that they lacked smartness I am not prepared to deny.

There are those who keep or used to keep their iron-heads black on principle, though exactly what principle I am not certain. Mr Herbert Fowler used to do so and so did Mr Robert Harris. The remark is attributed to Young Tommy Morris that the amateur too often took his eye off the ball because the shining head of the iron attracted that errant eye in the back swing. I can claim for myself no particular principle except that of saving trouble. And yet there is one eminently sound argument for black clubs. Water wears away a stone, or, if I may be allowed a quotation from Ovid (I have just found it in a dictionary), 'Consumitur annulus usu.' If a ring is worn thin by mere use, how much more is an ironhead worn thin by the vigorous sandpapering of generations of caddies? Many a good putting cleek has grown 'tinny' by cleaning and, having had to be reinforced by metal on the back, has lost something of its magic. That is the great advantage of rustless steel. The clubheads merely need wiping and retain at once their weight and their perpetually youthful bloom.

My three old clubs have set me dreaming all sorts of pleasant ancient dreams, and the least I can do out of gratitude is to give them an airing and to play a shot with them. Unfortunately I have not that indispensable requisite, a ball, but there is a kind lady in the house who is believed to possess one. Perhaps if I promised to play nothing but running shots up and down the lawn and not in the direction of the River Cam, which flows beside it, she would lend me that ball. I think I shall be very brave and ask her.

GAPS IN MY EDUCATION
(1945)

I was thinking a little sadly the other day about the gaps in my golfing education. I don't mean in the playing of the game because they are too vast and too obvious, but in the matter of British courses of a high class which I ought to have seen and have not. It is not a very long list and perhaps the fact that it is so comparatively short is evidence of a misspent life. I wish, however, that it was shorter still, for my pilgrimages are not now likely to be extensive and some of these courses will, humanly speaking, remain for ever unvisited. There are several in Scotland that really are gaps: Dornoch for instance, for which I once had all my plans set and then was prevented by a day of flood at St Andrews which postponed a championship. There are Brora, Nairn, in a lesser degree essential, and then two serious blots on my escutcheon in the west; I have never been either to Machrihanish or Islay; I have in my mind's eye a perfectly clear and erroneous picture of Mount Zion, Islay's famous hole, and the picture will never be corrected now.

In England and Wales I have less cause for shame. As regards famous seaside courses I believe I ought to have seen Pennard, near Swansea, since those who know it think almost unutterable things of it, but at least I am in the same boat in my ignorance with a great many other people.

Perhaps too I ought to have been to Bude, but the fact that I
have not brings no overwhelming sense of guilt. As to inland
courses, too, my conscience is fairly clear. Blackmoor in
Hampshire and Sherwood Forest in Nottinghamshire and
possibly Blackwell in Worcestershire—apart from those I
am, I honestly believe myself, tolerably well educated. I have
never been to the Channel Islands and I suppose Grouville
ought to be visited for Harry Vardon's sake, even as one
must cast reverent eyes on the now decayed glories of
Musselburgh, for the sake of the Parks and Dunns, Bob
Ferguson and the rest of its old heroes. Ireland, alas!
discloses the worst gap of all. I am almost ashamed to admit
that, though I once wrote a sufficiently vivid account of it in a
book, I have never been to Portrush. 'Is not the Giant's
Causeway worth seeing?' asked Boswell, and Dr Johnson
replied: 'Worth seeing? Yes: but not worth going to see.'
There was no golf in that part of the world then or perhaps
the great lexicographer would have answered differently. I
am sure Portrush must be worth going to see and I hope I
may yet do so. The air is said to be like a bottle of champagne
and that is now to one of my means almost unattainable in
any other way. And finally there is Lahinch which I imagine
—probably again I am quite wrong—full of the noblest
sandhills and dearest little nestling valleys conceivable.

No, the list is not, all things considered, very long; I have
been lucky and must be grateful. Photographs of golf
courses are the most futile things in the world. They seldom
give any real notion, even to those who know them, and to a
stranger they are useless; but without them one makes in
one's head imaginary pictures of unseen courses and they
are better than nothing. The odd thing is, at least in my
experience, that once the real place has been seen the
imaginary picture vanishes past recalling. I have often tried

to compare the real with the imaginary and have always failed. The fanciful picture is of the stuff of dreams and just melts away. It is mercifully otherwise with one's pictures of courses known long since, which have been rudely changed. I have several times played on Felixstowe as an eighteen-hole course and, with all respect to it, my recollections are rather shadowy; but, thank goodness, I have only to shut my eyes and see in almost every detail the nine-hole course that I played on, now sixty years since. There is even Willie Fernie in a yachting cap and shirt-sleeves outside his shop by the Martello Tower, waggling a half-made driver. It is the same at Sandwich. When I am actually on the spot I am hard put to it to find the hollow in which was the old seventeenth green, so overgrown is it with tangled grass. But here again let me shut my eyes and I see it all as clear as day, with my ball disappearing over the bank and myself hastening, as fast as dignity will allow, to find out what has happened on the further side. There was always the hope of a three, though it was usually the other and undeserving fellow whose ball lay dead.

There are visions of unvisited golf courses that are perhaps the most exciting of all, namely of those that are not courses yet but ought to be some day when we are all dead. I can think of four such places, each of which can still give me in imagination an exquisite thrill. Two are in Wales, one in the north and one in the south. The first is at Dyffryn in Merioneth where I was once taken by some enthusiastic pioneers. We walked over the little course then in existence, pleasant, sandy, with good sea turf, but in no way calculated to stir the blood. Then we stepped, as far as I remember, over a low sandhill, and behold, we were in a new and magical country of the most glorious hills and valleys and gorges and plateaux of sand that I had ever seen, stretching away into the distance. There was scarcely a blade of grass, nothing but pure, beautiful, undulating sand perfectly laid out by the hand of Providence, and if ever I wanted to be a millionaire it was then. Even a millionaire would, I take it, be hard put to it to clothe that vast expanse with turf and perhaps it will have to be left to higher powers, but some day there may be such a links there as never was seen, unless perhaps at my other Welsh paradise, the name of which is, I believe, Merthyr Mawr. That I have never explored and seen only from a car on the way from Southerndown to Porthcawl, but even a passing glance at it is enough to make any architect's mouth water.

Another such heaven-sent spot comes more dimly back to me from a visit of forty years ago to Lelant. It was, as I remember, over against that most engaging little course and its name was Hayle. There was turf there, too, and no need to wait for the work of the centuries, but as far as I know nothing has ever been done. Many have doubtless gazed on it 'with wild surmise,' but that is as far as they have ever gone.

Finally, in a lonely tract of country somewhere between Bury and Mildenhall there is to be seen perhaps the greatest marvel of all, a course that hardly needs making. The sand lies on the surface in ready-made bunkers; there is a row of fir trees just as at Worlington; the turf looks perfection; the land is flat, with here and there a gentle undulation. That is at least how I recall it. Distance may have lent a little enchantment to my view, but not, I am convinced, to any outrageous extent. At the time I exclaimed that here was another and a greater Worlington, and anyone who knows the profundity of my sentiments towards those noble nine holes will appreciate what I felt at that moment. Doubtless all those things are still there in their desolate beauty, scorned by the agriculturist, wasting their sweetness: or did I dream them? At any rate, I shall always hug the vision of them to myself. Perhaps that is one of the places that are best unvisited.

THE LAST BALL
(1946)

I have lately been told two stories as to the famine of golf balls. One is rather shameful and shows to what steps of degradation famine may drive a man. The other has a strictly honourable pathos. Let me get the worst one over first.

In a certain golf club there hung a club, having as I suppose, some history. It was given as a prize for a competition, and every year the winner suspended his victorious ball to it, even as is done with the President's Putter of the Society at Rye. It appears that the sight of these balls wasting their sweetness was too much for some poor wretch, who had lost his very last one in the rough. Wearing, presumably, a black vizard and at the dead of night, he unhooked the balls from their perch of honour, and next morning the club was found stripped of its ornaments. It is a really dreadful story. Even as the burgomaster in the famous play, after committing his murder, was forever hearing phantom bells, so I imagine criminal haunted by visions of golf balls dancing in the air before his conscience-stricken eyes.

My second story is of one whom I once saw play a crucial nineteenth hold for his school in the Halford Hewitt Cup at Deal. Then he was a subaltern with an alarming colonel for a partner. Now he is a colonel himself and has lately returned to golf after some six and a half years of soldiering. After a few games he was faced by the horrid fact of having but a single ball left for his next round. Musing gloomily on this state of things, be began to unpack some of his possessions that he had not seen for years, and among them a box containing some golfing oddments.

One of these was a cup that had been presented to him for doing a hole in one, and at the bottom of the cup nestled the very ball with which he had achieved it, a little yellow and faded but still of serviceable aspect. For a while he 'doubted in his abject spirit,' but the temptation was too great and it was with two balls in his pocket that he set out for his round at Wimbledon.

There were clearly too many trees at the first few holes and it was only when he came into the more open country that, not without some feeling of sacrilege, he teed his relic. The reader will here guess the end of the story, namely that the ball had grown old and torpid in the prison of its cup and would not fly. That might have been a proper punishment, but the reader has guessed wrongly. In fact, the ball flew 'with a divine click' and from that moment all went well till he found himself one up with three to play. The tee shot to the sixteenth, as many will know, is an exhilarating one, from a high place down into a valley with plenty of room. It inspired my colonel to hit his very best, and now he must play an iron shot to the plateau green perched defiantly in the corner, with a peril of woodland on the left. He hit out bravely as a soldier should and his iron shot was, as I gather, one of those which seem to us perfect when we are aiming at nothing in an open field but not so good when having any precise object. In short, it was hooked or, as he prefers to call it, 'too much held up'; it vanished into the trees and was never seen again.

It is a sad story but not an unheroic one. If a ball must die then it is a hundred times better that it should be lost from a manly hook than from a weak and ignoble slice. 'One crowded hour of glorious life' on the links is better than 'an age without a name' at the bottom of a cup, forgotten and unregarded. I cannot grieve overmuch on that sylvan tomb, though to be sure, if the colonel says I should think differently had it been my ball, he may be right. We can sometimes be wonderfully placid, waiting on a summer evening at a rustic station while a companion is telephoning madly down the line to retrieve a bag that has been carried on by the train. After all it is his luggage, not ours. Still I am rather sorry about that ball.

It was just after hearing this story that I read another in the newspaper about a precious ball. It seems that one of the green staff at St Andrews while re-facing a bunker on the Old Course, I think at the third hole, disinterred a hand-hammered gutty ball. It bore the name of the illustrious Willie Dunn, one of the twin brothers from Musselburgh who played the famous foursome against Allan Robertson and Tom Morris. My newspaper said that the ball must be a hundred years old. This is nearly but not, I think, quite true. I have been looking up my history and Mr James Balfour (Mr Leslie Balfour-Melville's father) in his reminiscences attributes the coming of the gutty ball to 'about the beginning of the year 1848.' He dated it from a match played at Blackheath by Admiral Maitland Dougall and Sir Ralph Anstruther against two others and recalls Sir Ralph's words: 'A most curious thing—here is a golf ball of gutta-percha; Maitland and I have played with it all day in the rain, and it flies better at the end of the day than it did at the beginning.'

That ball was, doubtless, one of the original smooth ones that flew better after a few hacks with an iron, and it was a little later, as we are told, that 'it occurred to an ingenious saddler in South Street to hammer them all round with the thin end of a hammer.' So we may say that this ball of Willie Dunn's is, at any rate, very well advanced in its nineties, if not quite yet a hundred years old. It is rather a pleasant fact that it was found in the face of a bunker. I imagine that its owner was playing a wooden club shot from close to the bunker and half-topped it so venomously that it embedded itself in the face too deeply to be retrieved. There it has been waiting ever since for some explorer to rescue it, and now it has found an honoured place in Royal and Ancient Club-house. How strange, but also how superior, it must feel among some of the curious mis-shapen weapons, the products of too ingenious inventors, barred by the Rules of Golf Committee, which puts them in a chamber of horrors of their own.

I have the greatest respect for my fellow-members; they are 'all, all honourable men,' but I hope the ball is safely guarded. There is no knowing what somebody might do, driven desperate by lack of ammunition, though he might find the ball rather flinty-hearted. I possess an early hand-hammered gutty of my own, which lives in a box with a feathery bearing the great name of Allan. I have played a shot or two with both of them, but only the very shortest and mildest of shots on the most open of lawns and even then I was frightened out of my wits lest I should socket it into a flower-bed, where it should bury itself for ever. So I don't think I shall be tempted to do anything rash, but after that first story of mine I do not propose to trust anyone else with them. This terrible ball-hunger may yet make thieves of the most unblemished of us.

THE GOLFER'S CIGARETTE
(1947)

At this time, when we are exhorted on patriotic grounds or compelled on economic ones to reduce our smoking, it may be appropriate to consider the question in relation to the golfer. The average golfer has acquired the habit of smoking a good deal in the course of his round. Sometimes in moments of crisis to soothe his agitated feelings, sometimes in exquisite surcease when the crisis is over; and, if he makes good resolutions, he will feel the want of tobacco fully as poignantly as any other man. I am not yet prepared to say from the evidence of my own eyes whether he has made, or rather whether he has kept, those resolutions. I am writing some little time after St Andrews and Carnoustie and trying to remember how much the players smoked.

Some of the American victors certainly seemed to me to light a good many cigarettes, but I am not sure that they smoked them to the end. I thought rather that they lighted them at crucial instants and then threw them away after a few relieving puffs as the illustrious Bobby Jones used to do. In any case, I fancy they had brought their own native brands with them and so could not lacerate Mr Dalton's feelings. I know that my old friend, Francis Ouimet, gave me several which did not emanate from this country. They were not Lucky Strikes, such as I had smoked in 1922, but they had much the same flavour and reminded me pleasantly of the National and the Country Club and the now remote days of the first match. As to our own players, they certainly had an occasional cigarette, but I would not go further than that in any generalisation. I can provide no damning evidence either for the Chancellor of the Exchequer or for those who are for ever trying to discover some reason, such as the lack of calories, why we lost, beyond the fact that the other side played just a bit better.

It is curious to remember that once upon a time, and not really so very long ago, it was not deemed the right thing to smoke in a match of importance. Freddie Tait was very fond of his pipe, but on a great occasion he would give it to a friend in the crowd to carry and take every now and then a few surreptitious puffs. I recall a story told me by an old friend now dead and a good Hoylake golfer in his day, Edmund Spencer, who was an inveterate smoker. He reached the last eight of the Amateur Championship at Muirfield in 1897, and while playing his final match heard an indignant Scottish spectator exclaim, 'I should like to knock his cigarette out of his mouth.' That was certainly an extreme view and already, I should have thought, a little out of date because another Hoylake golfer, Harold Hilton, had by that time become a familiar spectacle with his perpetual cigarette. At any rate, it is a good many years since smoking could be held to show any disrespect for an occasion or an opponent. If anything, it shows too great a respect rather than frivolity or lightness of heart.

There have been many great golfers who have been great smokers, but if I had to choose the three most famous and most typical I should say Harold Hilton for cigarettes, Ted Ray for pipes and Walter Travis for cigars. Ray's pipes were incidentally always a source of interest to me because they had, if I may so express it, curly shafts. I do not know how it may be with other people, but when I have tried to play with a pipe in my mouth I have always been afraid of hitting it with my arm, and with grave danger to my teeth, in the act of following through. That was with an ordinary straight pipe, and the danger would seem to be greater with a bent one. However, it did not seem to trouble Ray, who never took his pipe out of his mouth, and there was certainly no lack of rude vigour in his follow through. The cigar-smoking golfer has always been a comparative rarity, and Walter Travis's cigar created a great impression at Sandwich in 1904. It was such a very black and formidable cigar and accorded so perfectly with his rather sinister air. There seemed something as calculated and devilish about it as there was about those long putts that nothing could keep out of the hole. It made him look what he was, a killer.

For the ordinary mortal—and I am thinking of happier and cheaper days—a cigar has just the opposite significance. It stands for a jovial, post-prandial foursome, in which nothing greatly matters. There is about it an essential lack of seriousness. Either all is well with the world, or, if it is ill, it is so very ill that it is vain to repine. In an old article on golf at St Andrews (it was published in the *Cornhill* in 1867) there is an account of a foursome, in which two partners, Browne and Gurney by name, are not hitting it off very well, owing to Browne's habit of sending wild tee shots into the whins. There is 'another search, another ineffectual uprooting of a whin, and Gurney again emerges, but this time, wonderful to relate, with a comparatively cheerful countenance. He takes out his cigar-case, lights a cigar, and walks along contentedly smoking it, and apparently enjoying the scenery. This is a fatal sign. When a man smokes, he is either winning very easily or has given up all hope of winning.' Today that last statement may still be applied to cigars but not to smoking in general and assuredly not to a cigarette.

There is a great variety of golfing cigarettes. There is the one that a man lights on the tee just to steady him and help him over the first hole. There is the one, particularly applicable to medal rounds, which follows a disaster in a bunker leading to a six or a seven. There is, in a match, the one that is felt to be absolutely necessary when a nice little winning lead of three up or so has suddenly been reduced to a single hole. There is the cigarette to be smoked at the turn, irrespective of the state of the game, but because the turn is a definite occasion and an occasion calls for tobacco. Finally and most blissful is the dormy cigarette, when the player feels that

> *. . . nor steel, nor poison,*
> *Malice domestic, foreign levy, nothing,*
> *Can touch him further.*

There are doubtless many other kinds, for I have enumerated only five, and I heard a golfer of distinction admit the other day that he had smoked nine and twenty —and done a 74—before lunch. Let me hasten to add that it was also before the Budget. It is very hard to prove whether tobacco does us any good, but we think it does. Similarly those who have acquired, as I have, the habit of smoking while we write, think it helps us to find the right word. It may, in fact, be quite the wrong word, but we get along with the sentence which is hanging fire. We are like Charles Surface who said he never lost if he threw on a bottle of champagne, or at least that he never felt his losses. But today these are all academic questions since we are, of course, doing what Mr Dalton tells us.

REDUCTION OF ARMAMENTS
(1948)

For some little time I have been on the brink of writing about the recent proposal of the English Union that golf clubs should hold competitions in which the players are confined to an armoury of seven clubs apiece, in order to see how they fare and to compare notes as to the result. I have hesitated, partly because the topic of disarmament was not a wholly new one, though that might produce too many inhibitions; partly because it might be thought to have something to do with the rules. A burnt child dreads the fire, and I have had plenty of the rules in the last two years or more. Further, on any such subject a member of the Rules of Golf Committee who is also a writer on golf must in his dual capacity tread delicately. However, there is here as yet really no question of making new rules, though one might conceivably arise some day. So it is possible to treat the proposal simply as what it is, an experiment, and an interesting one.

As I have said, the reduction of armaments has been proposed before. By chance I found something I had written about it a dozen or more years ago. An old friend, and in his day a very good golfer, who gave up the game too early, Mr O. T. Falk, had then been writing to *The Times* suggesting legislation of a revolutionary character, whereby the permissible maximum should be three clubs. Today one of the chief arguments for reduction is a saving of expense, both in clubs and caddies. When Mr Falk wrote his letter some years before the war we all had more money wherewith to pay for clubs and caddies, and moreover both were much cheaper than today. He is a distinguished economist, and economic considerations were not, I think, absent from his mind, for he used some rather formidable expressions as to the 'reorganisation of the social structure' which might be expected to go much further than it had then gone. His main theme, however, was, I think, that golf would be a better, more skilful, and more interesting game, and he defined the effect of his proposal in an admirably precise sentence: 'Uniformity of the hitting method and great variety of clubface are replaced by greater or complete uniformity of clubface and variety of method of hitting.'

He even went so far as to urge that there was much to be said for only a single club. There, I fancy, few would agree with him, if only because the sole club would of necessity be an iron, and golf without the joy of wooden clubs would be a truly drab affair. Before the war there was a young lady who used to play in the ladies' championship with a single cleek, but, though her skill with it was considerable, she had no imitators; nor, when the novelty had worn off, did she cause much interest. To most of us, if we played with a single club, might be adapted Dr Johnson's remark: 'Sir, a woman's preaching is like a dog's walking on his hind legs. It is not done well; but you are surprised to find it done at all.'

Even a reduction to three clubs struck me as far too drastic to make any converts, and I see that I expressed the wish that he had said five or six, and six for choice. No doubt Mr John Ball could play pitches with a moderately straight-faced iron, and get out of bunkers with it, but he was above ordinary laws. No doubt Douglas Rolland, as I read lately in an article by Mr Longhurst, may have carried for a casual game no more than three clubs and so used his driving cleek as a putter. But he was a casual genius and not, moreover, a very good putter. No, golfers in general want a putter to putt with and some club made for the purpose with which to get out of bunkers. In the maximum of seven clubs now suggested there is room for both.

Just as children play a game of thinking what they would like for dinner on some special occasion, so many golfers are probably now playing a game of thinking which are the seven clubs they would choose. I am too obsolete a golfer for my experience to be worth giving; still, for what it is worth, I give it. At Aldeburgh last summer I two or three times played nine holes and carried almost the entire armoury I now possess—a brassie, a spoon, a putter, irons No. 3, No. 4, No. 5, and a mashie-niblick, as to the number of which I feel uncertain. There were seven clubs, and I cannot honestly assert that I felt the need for any more. I wanted that which was past praying for, clubs that would hit the ball a great deal farther, but I did not want more clubs.

A brassie to drive with is, to be sure, a personal idiosyncrasy; most people would no doubt take up a driver instead and possibly a driver with a comparatively shallow face so that they might, if need be, use it through the green. Indeed, if the number of iron clubs were limited I fancy that there would be a general move in favour of shallower faces, and further that many golfers would find them easier to play with. As to the irons, I suggest that the No. 4 is almost a superfluous luxury, but it does for many supply a felt want, not so much in point of distance as in the playing of running shots. It is rather like that very old friend that used to be called an 'approaching cleek,' or more familiarly a 'jigger.'

The shot can be played with other clubs, of course, but that comparatively narrow-faced iron was a trusty ally.

It is quite clear that many golfers would be heart-broken at the thought of parting with their niblicks, and no doubt the modern niblick or wedge (I am old-fashioned enough to wish it had never been invented) does produce wonderful results out of bunkers. If they are going to carry one, and also a mashie-niblick for their pitching, then they will have, as far as I can see, to be content with an iron and a mashie (No. 3 and No. 5) and leave their No. 4 behind. Here may be a serious question which some will solve one way and some another, but whatever they decide I am not going to shed many tears on their behalf. They ought to get along pretty well, and so they will if they set out with an open mind and do not spend their time in vain regrets.

I could wish that these tentative competitions could have been held in other than wintry weather. Courses naturally tend to be slow, heavy and long in winter and scores to be higher. There will be no harm in that if players make due allowance for that obvious fact, but clearly they must not compare the scores they do now with those they have done in summer and then lay the blame on their reduced armaments. Their comparisons must be with their scores made under similar conditions, and then I do not think they will find much difference. I hope and believe that they will find the game very good fun and very interesting in the matter of improvising shots; that, in short, it will blend instruction with amusement.

Whether the results of this experiment can ever lead to limitation by rule of the number of clubs I do not profess to know. If ever it did there would be grave matters to be considered such as its effect on the players from other countries who come to play with us here and also upon what may be called 'vested interests,' the interests of those who make clubs, and of professionals who use them to gain fame and reward by doing the lowest scores they possibly can. With these last I should not have too much sympathy, especially as they would learn to adapt themselves to new conditions more quickly and skilfully than would anybody else. It is the ordinary amateurs, and especially the young amateurs, who would benefit economically at any rate from such a rule, and they are the people chiefly to be considered. However, that is probably afar off. Let us see first how the experiment works, and let us hope that it has a good trial.

SILENCE IS GOLDEN
(1949)

There is no rule of golf laying down what one may or may not say to one's opponent, but I gather from a paragraph that I have just read that it is otherwise at Association football. No referee can insist upon the game being played in absolute silence, and a player can call out to one of his own side 'so long as he uses no ungentlemanly expression.' On the other hand, if he calls out to one of the other side, and so causes his attention to be distracted, dire things can befall him. He may be deemed guilty of ungentlemanly conduct, he may be cautioned and finally 'an indirect free kick' (I am not learned enough to know what that means) may be ordered. Here is an example which will make an instant appeal to a friend of mine. The one rule of all rules of golf that he really wants made is to deal with the opponent who says, 'I am afraid that at this stage of the match I must ask you to hole that one.' I am not sure what the penalty is to be, probably 'something lingering, with boiling oil.' Generally speaking he wants the wretch to lose the hole and match, to be disqualified, kicked out of the club, blackballed for all other clubs, and in short, wiped off the face of the earth.

I agree with him that the offence is a heinous one, but I think that perhaps he underestimates the difficulty of drafting a rule to meet it. What, for instance, is the exact form of words to be penalised? 'I should like to give you that one, but I mustn't,' is, for instance, a variant equally criminal. I remember it, sad to say, being used on the last green in a championship, and with the natural—I refrain from saying the desired—result: the putt was ruined, and the villain, unconscious or deliberate, went on to win at the nineteenth or twentieth. To hole the first of two short putts and exclaim in an ecstasy of relief 'First half,' is another action wholly to be deprecated, and it is conceivable that some form of words might be devised against such remarks, or indeed against any remark at all made before the opponent plays his putt. I do not think it would be wise, though it would no doubt be possible.

There is, however, a good deal to be done without any speech at all, and I have a shameful feeling that I may have done it myself. The mere looking at the other fellow's putt, as if debating whether to give it to him or not, does not improve his frame of mind or his chances of holing it, and yet we have most of us probably been guilty. I remember that in wartime some evacuees insisted on leaving their comfortable place of refuge and returning to the danger zone on the ground that they did not like 'the way the butler looked,' and the way some people look at our putts is in the highest degree objectionable. I have seen people of the most incontestable honour hole their own putt, extend a club to the enemy's ball as if about to knock it away, and then think better of this generous impulse. There is no legislation possible against such deeds, which are indeed done quite unconsciously. For that matter the really dreadful remark which I began by quoting may proceed from the agitation of the moment, or a sadly mistaken notion of politeness. There is, I am afraid, nothing to be done save to try hard not to do these things ourselves, and never again to play with anybody who does them more than once. As with a dog, a first bite may be allowed, but that is all.

I recall the late Sir Ernley Blackwell, a great stickler for the observation of rules, and a man of the most perfect golfing manners, saying 'If a man looks to see whether he has laid me a stymie I consider it an impertinence.' That is a truly formidable expression, but there are occasions on which it is justified. I suppose there is no one who, as he sees his ball apparently blocking his opponent's way, has not taken a mere passing glance to discover how effective is the blockade. That is only human, but if an opponent, having laid us a stymie, takes a prolonged survey of the situation, perhaps going down on hands and knees to that end, he is fully worthy of Sir Ernley's condemnation. There is only one further offence that he can commit: he can say, 'I don't think it's a stymie. I've left you room.' For that it seems to us at the moment that even his heart's blood would not atone.

The putting green is the most prolific scene of what those so scrupulous football players would call ungentlemanly conduct, but there are other occasions. To stand too closely over an opponent in a bunker is either an act of utter ghoulishness or implies an offensive doubt of his veracity. As Horace Hutchinson once very properly wrote, 'There is no justification for the audible enumeration one by one of his strokes,' and in this matter of enumeration there is no one that I have more whole-heartedly desired to kill than he who, in a friendly match, insists on writing down my score in a horrid little book. If he wants to keep his own he must be allowed to do so, but why should he unasked keep mine? He is the kind of man of whom it was once said, 'When I play with So-and-so I always leave my niblick behind.' Well, well, that is one of the things that can never happen to me again. A very famous judge once said to a friend of mine: 'I am afraid when I was at the Bar I must have done many improper things; in fact, I know I did.' So I know I did many improper and highly irritating things when I played golf, and it is some little comfort for playing no more that I cannot now be guilty.

There still remains, however, the risk of saying improper things as a spectator, and that I shall doubtless continue to do. One who once played for Oxford and is now a distinguished KC still reproaches me with something I said when he put his second shot at the home hole through the clubhouse window at Rye in the University match. Upon the honour of a poor gentleman I did not mean him to hear it, but I doubt if he quite believes me, and at any rate that is no excuse; he did hear me. Some spectators' voices (mine no doubt among them) have an unfortunate power of carrying. The thought of Rye brings back to me the sound of Arthur Croome's voice growling away in the distance as I am trying to play a critical shot. He was wholly unconscious and he spoke low, but the carry of his voice was immense. How pleasant if only one could hear it again.

There is nothing to be done to spectators, not even a free kick. I remember some long time ago that in a professional tournament, I think at Gleneagles, the marker made a mistake in the cards of two eminent players, putting down a four to X and a five to Y at a particular hole instead of vice-versa. Everybody, players, spectators and all, were certain as to the fact and there arose some question as to what was to be done. Then up spoke one who was, incidentally, a member of the Rules of Golf Committee. 'It's perfectly simple,' he said, 'you disqualify the marker.' On the same principle you might no doubt disqualify the spectator. More effective than that, you might warn him off the course, as delinquents in the world of horses are warned off

Newmarket Heath. That is an alarming thought. I must mind my 'p's' and 'q's' and maintain the most discreet silence, lest I be escorted off the links by a guard armed with blasters. I really shall try to behave myself.

LOCAL RULES FOR TIGERS
(1950)

The reader may have gathered from an occasional remark that I have had all I want of the rules of golf and that since I retired from the committee into private life I am not easily to be drawn on the subject. Now and again, however, my interest is aroused even on that well-worn theme and nobody could resist the proposed local rule of which I have just heard from a friend in India: 'A ball lying in a tiger's pugmark on the brown may be lifted and placed without penalty.'

This is not a joke; the tiger is not of the two-legged kind, but the genuine article, and the course is that of Kodaikanal in southern India, a hill station of Madras. It is, I believe, eighteen years and more since I wrote some account of the course in *Country Life*. Save that browns take the place of greens, the course looks for all the world as if it were in Surrey, perhaps near Woking and Worplesdon and West Hill, with its light green fairways and its dark green fir trees. I fancy there is also mimosa, represented by a thick yellow line between the two shades of green on the club tie, which I wear proudly as an honorary member, though an absentee one.

In that article I mentioned that tigers occasionally played on the course, but I gather that this had become a thing of the past until quite lately, when they have come back. Apparently, the owners of the cattle and the cowherds had formed a habit of leaving a few buffaloes or cows to graze on the course at night and this was too obvious a temptation for the tigers, which had been driven to the hills by the failure of the rains and the lack of water lower down.

In the course of time three of these marauders were shot, one of them within fifty yards of the second hole, whither he had come back to his kill. However, that was not the end, and I shall quote from my friend's letter; 'Last Sunday evening there was heavy rain and, while it was still raining, two buffaloes were seen by the club servants, galloping past the clubhouse, which indicated clearly that something was after them, as ordinarily buffaloes are the most lethargic of animals.

'Anyhow, some time during the night a tiger wandered on to the eighteenth brown, which after the rain was very soft, and left very clear and deep impressions on it. The next night he was again on the prowl and left other pugmarks on the sixth and fifteenth browns, which are fairly close to each other; but this time there were small pugmarks as well, which showed that the prowlers were a tigress accompanied by her cubs.'

The little tiger being brought out for a walk by its mamma is rather engaging. Yet on the whole I should prefer to play my golf where there are rather fewer tigers. In fact, when I first read my friend's letter I felt a distinctly cold shiver run down my back, just as I do whenever I re-read *The Hound of the Baskervilles* and come to Dr Mortimer saying in a whisper, 'Mr Holmes, they were the footprints of a gigantic hound.'

Use and wont doubtless make a difference and my friend does not seem to have minded the tigers so much as he did the inquisitive people who came to gaze at their pugmarks. He counted fifteen cars on the road just above the eighteenth brown and about fifty people crowding on to it. This, he remarks, was 'too much of a good thing'; he drove the crowd away and had the exciting marks rubbed out so that there should be nothing to see. I sincerely hope that the suggested local rule has not since then been required, for I am bound to say that the thought of a tiger lurking in the rough would, I feel sure, put me completely off my game. My only experience of the kind—and it was infinitely milder—was with the fierce wolfish dogs in the nature of Alsatians to be found in Macedonia. Near one of the greens on our course there was a peasant's shack which harboured two or three of these creatures. They did no more than look at us with very ugly faces, but they had an unattractive habit of creeping rather nearer to us from behind while we were waggling. One of my regular opponents had a most elaborate preliminary address to the ball and definitely needed a sentry. One or two of these Macedonian dogs might have hastened some of the more dilatory putters at St Andrews the other day.

My story from Kodaikanal has sent me off at a tangent to wondering when 'tiger' was first used by golfers to signify an eminent person with a handicap of plus something. I am quite sure it was never heard in the remote days when I began to play golf, nor indeed for some time afterwards. Neither was 'rabbit' in use; the humbler members of the golfing creation were, to the best of my belief, described as duffers. 'Tiger' has certainly had quite other meanings in earlier times. It signified the small groom who accompanied his master in a dog-cart. For instance, Bailey Junior was Mr Montague Tigg's, or rather Mr Tigg Montague's, tiger in *Martin Chuzzlewit*. The word also signified a disreputable person, a flash man, 'a dissolute swaggerer or bully,' in the language of the *Oxford Dictionary*. Let me cite a venerable friend, Major Pendennis, on the subject of Mr Bloundell-Bloundell: 'A man may have a very good coat-of-arms, and be a tiger, my boy,' he remarked to his nephew. 'That man is a tiger, mark my word—a low man . . . He frequents low gambling-houses and billiard halls, sir, he haunts third-rate clubs—I know he does.' I have consulted a new and fascinating book, Mr Eric Partridge's *Dictionary of the Underworld*, in which is to be found the language of spivs and gangsters and racketeers and such like more or less, perhaps rather less, attractive people. 'Tiger' can, it appears, mean a parasite, but this is slang and not cant. It is also gamblers' slang for the game of faro and tiger-juice is a bootlegger term for whisky.

Nowhere can I find any clue to the modern golfing meaning of 'tiger.' Can it be that the word was originally applied to one who like Mr Bloundell-Bloundell was far too good a player for anyone to play with safely and that gradually it came to have a more innocent meaning? This is a pure guess on my part and probably a bad one. I rather incline to believe that the tiger was chosen simply as the most obvious opposite of the mild or harmless rabbit. Perhaps someone can tell me and meanwhile I am glad the tiger is a strictly metaphorical animal in this country.

DEATH TO THE TOPPER
(1951)

Now and again one comes across a passage about the game of golf that seems so archaic that it must surely have been written in prehistoric ages. Then one discovers with a most painful shock that, at the time it was published, one was oneself already a golfer of some years' experience and with a certain conceit of oneself and one's game. 'Good heavens,' one exclaims. 'Did I subscribe to these astonishing sentiments? Can it be that I might even have talked such nonsense myself?'

These, or something like them, were my feelings the other day when I lighted on a book in my shelves that to the best of my knowledge I had never read before and had even forgotten I possessed. It is about fifty-three years old, and the particular passage that staggered me was in a chapter on the making the keeping of courses. 'As a general principle,' says the author, 'at every hole, except on the putting green where it brings its own reward, a bad shot should be followed by a bad lie and a good shot should be correspondingly rewarded by a good one.' He admits that this is a counsel of perfection not invariably to be attained and then proceeds: 'But there is one kind of bad stroke which by universal consent must be summarily punished, whenever and wherever it is perpetrated, and that is a "topped shot". The reasons for this are obvious.'

Such a dreadful state of things must never be allowed that the player should suffer no disadvantage from his mistake. 'Wherefore, in making your first tee select a spot some sixty yards in front of which a yawning bunker stretches right across the course, and if it be so narrow, or so shallow, that a topped ball will jump over it or run through it, dig it wider and deeper, so that all balls crossing its jaws will inevitably be swallowed up.' That is fierce enough, but observe the truly remarkable words that follow: 'If no bunker is to be had a pond will do equally well, or a railway, or a hedge, or a wall—anything in short that is impassable.' And this, as I venture to call it, surprising nonsense was written not by one but lately introduced to the game on some cockney meadow, but by a good Scotsman, brought up by the sea in his native country and no mean player. What is not surprising, after reading it, is that there were so many shockingly bad 'steeple-chase' holes laid out about that time.

Even so, I cannot help thinking that our author's punitive enthusiasm, his resolution that the wretched topper should be engulfed, rather ran away with him. I have been going through the courses of my acquaintance—and my knowledge, if far from 'peculiar,' is at least 'extensive'—and I cannot recall a single one in which the player is faced by a wall on the first teeing ground. I certainly do remember a wall in front of the second tee at beloved and departed Chiswick, quite a high wall and quite near the tee, and it belonged not inappropriately to a lunatic asylum. No denizen ever looked over it and said, as did the lunatic in Phil May's picture, 'Come in here,' but I really do not think a point blank attack on a wall makes a good tee-shot. There was once a wall, a very famous wall, to be carried with the drive to the fourth hole at Prestwick, but it was 'only a very little one', and below the level of the teeing ground.

Then again the author suggests a railway to carry from the first tee. That is surely rare. There is to be sure many a course fringed by a railway line, but I cannot for the life of me recall a single one where a shot has to be played over it. All the railway lines that I know are in the nature of lateral hazards. There was once, indeed, an exception of this rule in the seventh hole on the Dudular Course in Macedonia, of which I was myself the architect. The railway provided a capital diagonal tee-shot, but then this was not a crowded course, nor did many trains pass along that railway line. I cannot think of a single first hole with a frontal attack to be made on a hedge, though I do recall one with a ploughed field, namely our first hole at Eton, going in the direction of Cuckoo Weir; but that again was hardly a model course, though I spent many happy hours upon it. As to a pond, it is hard to imagine any hazard that would more effectively delay the start on a crowded morning, by reason of everyone fishing for his lost ball.

I think that even at his own date our author held rather curious views and must have felt that the first hole on many courses did not at all come up to his requirements. What of St Andrews or Hoylake or Prestwick, to name but three illustrious courses? The golfer could then, even as he can now, commit the high crime and misdemeanour of topping more or less with impunity. Westward Ho! had the black and oozy water of its flatteringly named 'burn' and Sandwich had rushes that have long since been hacked to pieces by furious niblicks, but generally speaking the start from the first tee was very wisely not made too alarming. Green committees, more charitable than our bloodthirsty author, seldom left 'a solid belt of gorse all across the course about sixty yards from the first tee.'

There are one or two fine courses which start with fine,

big bunkers bang in front of the first tee, such as those two neighbours, Hunstanton and Brancaster, the scenes of this year's English Championship. I have a dim recollection of a bunker in front of the first tee on the old nine-hole course at Felixstowe, but as I was only eight or nine years old at the time, it is probably not so large as I remember it. Those two in Norfolk are capital bunkers and it would have been a shame to waste them, but it would have been better if geography had allowed them to come later in the course. Even the most virtuous of men may top his first tee-shot when he feels very stiff on a bitterly cold morning. Do not let us be too hard on him.

It seems to me odd that my author was so utterly relentless towards the topper, for he wrote in gutty days. It was much easier to top the gutty than the rubber-core, it did not go nearly so far when it was topped, and it might bear such a deep scar from that one mistake as not to be of much service afterwards. If the author had been similarly malignant about the Haskell that went bounding along over hill and dale I should have had more sympathy with him.

I do not know whether it was that we were most of us rather bad players in the 'nineties, but I do know that we were much more afraid of topping. Cader, the short hole at Aberdovey, now regarded as 'just a blind mashie-shot over a sand hill' inspired everyone with terror. 'How did you go on at Cader?' was almost common form as a greeting. The more I think of it the more I am convinced that my author's views were both brutal and absurd. Topping is a manly weakness. The very greatest of men, men who could never play a feeble shot, can yet now and then hit a tee-shot bang on the top. I have seen them do it—yes, the very greatest of all.

ALIEN CLUBS
(1952)

I began my last week's article with a reference to Addington, and, behold, on the very night it was written came the burning of the clubhouse there! Everybody must feel sympathy with golfers thus bereft of their home, and in particular with those whose clubs had been left there and so were consumed. To lose a whole bag of clubs will always be tragic, and today it must be worse than ever on the purely economic grounds that they cost so much to replace. Long, happy years ago one could buy a club or two out of income whenever one had the mind; today a new set must amount to a capital expenditure. But it is, of course, the loss of cherished and trusty allies that is the really harrowing part of it. But yesterday they were things of beauty; the sheen of them 'was like stars on the sea'; today they are no more than blackened and twisted bits of metal. Those that were the oldest friends possibly came from the days before the invasion of steel shafts—a putter, perhaps, or a faithful little 'Sammy' or a 'Benny'; each of them had its individual pedigree and history; it had come from a famous man's shop, or, perhaps, at a great price from the champion's own playing set—the gap left by such a friend as that no other club can quite fill.

Such old favourites are now, however, growing rare; they

are to be found as pensioned veterans in cupboards rather than on active service in bags. So let us hope that not many of them are lost. Clubs that are bought and sold in sets, though of admirable workmanship and better than were their predecessors, cannot wind themselves round the heart in quite the same way. No one of them is unique, and however excellent each is yet only one of a class. To replace them will doubless cost much pure gold, but another set almost as like the last one as one pea is to another will surely be found. This is, I think, particularly true of irons. Even before this mass-produced age it was always much easier to use another man's irons than his driver or brassie, and still today there is more individual feeling and character about wooden clubs; they will always be the harder for which to find substitutes.

Sad as it is to lose old clubs, it is pleasantly exciting to obtain fresh ones, and, assuming him providently insured or wallowing in riches, I can almost find myself envying the man who must begin golfing life all over again with a brand new set. What fun he will have and how he will waggle those glittering baubles till he scarcely knows whether he is on his head or his heels! One piece of advice I venture to give him, namely that he should do his waggling on the turf and not merely on the floor of a shop. There is something about a shop, and particularly a great store, which will make 'his judgment go out a wisitin,' to use Mr Weller's expressive words, and he may find that he can scarcely recognise on the morrow the club that has enchanted him today.

Let me reinforce this advice by that of someone much better worth listening to, Harold Hilton. After saying that artificial light invests a club with some spurious glamour, he goes on, 'I have learnt my lesson, and nowadays I never buy a club except in daylight, and moreover I try to avoid buying a club within the precincts of a domicile or a clubhouse, as clubs have a habit of appearing at their very best when reposing for inspection on a carpet or even on oil-cloth. If I were in the business I should certainly cover the floor of my showroom with a thick, heavy carpet. The carpet might cost money, but I should possibly get rid of many ugly ducklings thereby.'

Though it is on the whole a sad thing to lose clubs, it is surely remarkable how many people do lose them—and yet perhaps it is not so remarkable considering how ladies leave diamond tiaras and diplomatists the most secret papers in taxis. At any rate the strange thing does occur and that often. I happened the other day on something I had written about sixteen years ago, on coming across an advertisement from a Railway Lost Property Depot. There were offered for sale at prices between a guinea (£1.05) and twenty-five shillings (£1.25) apiece 'forty sets of modern golf clubs'; and to make the offer more inviting they were 'all guaranteed.' What they were guaranteed to do I have no evidence, but if it was to make all the purchasers' shots successful, then it was an example of the dashing quality of private enterprise; I fancy a nationalised railway would be more cautious.

What puzzled me then and puzzles me now is not so much why the owners lost them—anybody can leave things behind in a railway carriage—as why they did not take the trouble to get them back. Some of them may have been so disgusted with their play that day that they resolved to give up the game, and so deliberately left their clubs as people sometimes leave unwanted babies on the rack. Perchance they left them in the cloakroom, meaning to reclaim them, and then something happened that changed the whole course of their lives so that they never came back. Did they elope? Were they suddenly moved to empty the till and decamp? They can scarcely have forgotten them, and yet there were those forty sets that had waited and waited for their faithless owners. I have sometimes seen and even been tempted by bundles of old clubs exposed outside a pawnbroker's shop. The reason why they have never been reclaimed is all too plain, but that railway treasure trove remains something of a mystery.

Incidentally, since everything to do with golf has now grown so dear, might not some of this lost legion of clubs be cheaply let out to those who want to play a round and have no clubs or, at any rate, none with them? A friend told me the other day that at municipal courses in Scotland the visitor often hires clubs. In particular he told me of a friend of his who had done so, appropriately enough, at Aberdeen, and paid an extremely small sum for the loan of some half-dozen clubs. It may be that this is a perfectly well-known custom on public courses and that I am simply ignorant and behind the times. At any rate it sounds a good plan and one might find in that job lot the magic wand for which one had been searching for years.

A borrowed club will sometimes do wonders, and then the borrower insinuates as clearly as he can, without actual mendicancy, that he would like to keep it, and the lender must either harden his heart or give way with the best grace he can muster. Douglas Rolland had a habit of arriving without any clubs for an exhibition match and borrowing a few with which he performed prodigies; but the really historic example of borrowed clubs is Walter Tavis's victory in our Amateur Championship in 1904. He had been putting very badly and almost at the last moment he borrowed from a compatriot the Schenectady putter which thereupon became famous. He also used a spoon that Ben Sayers insisted on lending him, and, if it was not so conspicuously deadly as the putter, it yet did great deeds. I can still remember as vividly as possible two shots that Travis played in the final with that spoon, one up to the second hole against the wind and another at the twelfth. They were played with a masterly control that remains unforgettable.

I, too, borrowed a spoon once, and for a little while did great things with it. This was in Macedonia. The spoon belonged to a hospital nurse and was lent to me through a third party. She was at once a generous and a hard-hearted lady; generous for trusting me with so rare a club, in a land where they were hard to come by; hard-hearted on demanding its return when I had grown so fond of it. Unfortunately I had written rather scornfully about the golfcourse at her hospital and those who played on it. I suppose she was justified, but I have never quite forgiven nor forgotten. It was a really exquisite spoon.

GUIDED MISSILES
(1953)

When this number of *Country Life* appears the Amateur Championship will have run half its course at Hoylake and, if all is well, I shall be there to watch it. Doubtless I shall see many interesting things and remarkable shots, but there is one thing I am pretty sure I shall not see, namely, a player doing a hole in one in each of four consecutive rounds. Yet that is what a lady, Mrs Small by name, and incidentally a grandmother, has lately done in New Zealand. What is more, she has holed her tee-shot seven times in all between January 15 of this year and April 19. A kind correspondent in New Zealand has sent me two newspaper cuttings on the subject and assures me that there is no possible doubt about the *bona fides* of the achievement. I should not dream of suggesting that there was. I entirely accept the lady's own simple explanation that 'she hits very straight shots, but her success is just due to an extraordinary run of luck.'

One of my two cuttings has the felicitous headline which I have stolen for this article, and the story is so astonishing that it may be set out in some detail. Mrs Small, who has a modest handicap of 17, plays at the Queen's Park Ladies' Golf Club at Invercargill, and she has done all her seven ones on that course. The reader may at once think—the idea occurred to me—that they were all done at one hole,

where there is some peculiarity in the green causing the ball
to run into the hole. I have seen such a green, and I
remember one in Wales, where throughout the whole day
in a meeting one player after another came prodigiously
excited into the clubhouse announcing that he had holed his
second shot at this particular hole.

That explanation will not do here. All holes at Invercargill
have names, a pleasant custom now growing all too rare, and
of Mrs Small's first half-dozen ones, two were achieved at
Waihopai (190 yards long), two at Polygon (135 yards), and
one each at Westward Ho! (114 yards) and Feldwick (135
yards). She also seems to have hit the flag at Westward Ho!
and was thought very unlucky not to have holed out, but this
was before holing had become a habit.

Three of these ones were done in consecutive rounds; the
fourth was intensely dramatic. One of the players who were
playing in front of her, having just putted out at Polygon,
said, 'Wait a minute; that's Mrs Small behind us, who holes
out in one. Let's see if she can do it again.' Whereupon Mrs
Small duly obliged; in went the ball with perfect docility. On
two of the four occasions she was playing with her husband,
on the other two with somebody else. After the fourth she
seems to have gone away for a little holiday, perhaps needing
a rest, and so was out of practice at doing ones when she
came home again. That made no difference; she went out to
play with her husband and a lady friend, and when they
reached the shortest hole on the course, Westward Ho!,
down she went again. The lady playing with her had possibly
been a little sceptical, for now she remarked, 'Seeing is
believing.'

What has happened since I do not know. When I told this
story to a lady of my acquaintance, she asked, 'Did she mean
to do it?' and was pained and surprised when I burst into an

unmannerly guffaw. Yet I suppose that, though we all mean to hole our tee-shot at a short hole, in the sense of hoping to do so, the notion of actually achieving it is seldom present in our mind. When Mrs Small gets on to the tee, she can hardly refrain from thinking about yet another one. Whether this would be a help or a hindrance one can hardly say without personal experience, but it certainly seems to have been a help to her. Finally the ones have not helped her to return any outstanding score for the entire round, and her handicap is still what it was before the run of luck began, namely 17. And to think that Harry Vardon did only a single hole in one and John Ball never did one at all! Certainly Fortune does distribute these favours unevenly. There is a temptation to dive into my trusty friend, *The Golfer's Handbook*, and set out all manner of statistics, but it seems at once rather lazy and unsportsmanlike; they are all in that admirable work if anyone wants them. Mrs Small is certain of her niche in the next edition.

Holes done in one when the shot from the tee was a blind one were always a little suspect when the caddie went forward to the green and hoped for the traditional bottle of whisky. Today, with so few caddies and whisky at its present price, the number of ones may have dropped. In this respect a scene comes back to me from a blind hole of some fame, Cader, now the third, but once the fourth, hole at Aberdovey. It was, I think, during our first summer meeting, 'way back' in 1892. A stout colonel drove off and had palpably sliced far away towards cover point. Yet the ball was found at the bottom of the hole. The colonel himself put forward no claim, but there the ball mysteriously was. A crowd seemed to collect from nowhere, as it always does when anything exciting happens, and in the midst of it I see a very small boy being kindly but firmly cross examined by my uncle, the president of the club. For a long time he stoutly maintains his innocence, then bursts into a flood of tears and confesses all. I do not think he had any mercenary motives; he had done it from pure loyalty to his employer and a generous desire to please.

Nearly everybody has holed his tee-shot once. I asked a friend of mine the other day how many times he had done it and he answered a little sadly, 'Only once'; but then, lest I should think meanly of him, he went on to explain that he had done equivalent deeds through the green. 'I have,' he said with a modest pride, 'holed a brassie shot.' He is a class above me there, in the same distinguished category with Gene Sarazen, who once won the Master's Tournament at Augusta, Georgia, by holding a wooden-club shot. Not at the home hole admittedly; that would be too much for the reader to believe, whose faith has already been severely tried in this article, but at the fifteenth. Gene has a whole chapter devoted to it in his book, under the heading *The Double Eagle*. He heard the applause greeting Craig Wood's finish on the home green and calculated that he wanted four threes to beat him. The par of the four holes was 5, 3, 4, 4, so that the outlook was definitely unpromising. However, he began by holing out for a two from 235 yards with his No. 4 wood, did the next three holes in the par score to tie with Wood, and he beat him next day on the play-off. So my statement was, as the reader will own, reasonably correct.

By far the most exciting thing that I, or perhaps anyone else, every saw very nearly happen in a British championship was at Hoylake in 1947. That was Frank Stranahan's finish in Fred Daly's year. He needed a four and a three to tie, took five at the seventeenth and then put his second within three or four inches of the home hole. I can still see that ball wriggling and biting its way into the turf, as if struggling to

force its way into the hole. If that ball had gone in ...
However, it did not, but it was a very close-run thing, and if
it had Jock Hutchison's one at the eighth hole at St Andrews,
when he tied with Roger Wethered and won the play-off,
would have seemed almost common-place.

Yet all these great players pale their ineffectual fires
before Mrs Small. My cutting tells me that after she had
done her seventh one she 'was not over-excited, but wondered when other Invercargill players were going to start
holing their tee-shots.' I cannot help feeling that Invercargill
has had its ration.

GOLF AND GERONTOLOGY
(1954)

The members of the recent International Conference on Gerontology did not, as far as I know, concern themselves with the achievements of elderly golfers. That seems a pity, for here is a piece of news that would have stirred them to their depths. A kind friend, who boasts himself a Jerseyman, has sent me a cutting from the *Jersey Weekly Post*, recording the feat of a very old friend of mine and of many golfers, Michael Scott. He was born in 1878, which, as I know painfully well, is some time ago. The other day he led a team of the Royal Jersey Club against the Jersey Eastern Golf Clubs. It was a thoroughly unpleasant, un-gerontological day of driving rain and a high wind. In the foursomes he played with Donald Ashton, one of the stalwarts of the Old Harrovian team at Deal, and they beat the top pair of the opposing side at the last hole. In the afternoon he really let himself go and crashed some wretched adversary, possibly too young to stand up against the weather, by 5 and 3.

Now that is surely a remarkable performance for one who has been a senior for twenty-one years and is today in the ultimate class of that society, beyond which there is no reckoning. Whether in point of skill or endurance or sheer enthusiasm for the game it seems to me a prodigious effort. Michael has always done things late. Though he had been a very fine golfer from his youth up (his family had a course at its own door at Stowell Park), and had begun winning championships with the Australian Open exactly fifty years ago, in 1904, he postponed his victory in our Amateur Championship at Hoylake till he was within a few weeks of being a senior in 1933. I never saw him play when he was quite young; I think almost the first time I met him was when he came home from Australia and first played for England against Scotland in 1911. I fancy that when he was younger he had had a comparatively long swing, more like that of his brother Osmund and his sister Lady Margaret; but I may be wrong. At any rate, when I first saw him he had the comparatively short, almost clipped swing, which hits the ball so crisply and sends it boring through the wind like an arrow. No one ever stood more firmly on his feet and his iron shots and cleek shots—he was a master of that now atrophied club—were, and I have no doubt still are, a joy to see.

My cutting says that he has lost some of his length and, being human, I suppose he must have, but that so-characteristic style of his and his imperishable keenness have served him well. I am not going to set out all his achievements. Are they not written—a long list of them—in the Who's Who of *The Golfer's Handbook?* I observe, incidentally, that he has done six holes in one. Did I not say that he was a good iron player? He now lives in the Channel Islands and I send him my warmest greetings and congratulations across the sundering seas. As the cabman said of the intoxicated gentleman on the pavement, in John Leech's old *Punch* picture, 'I only wish I had half his complaint.'

The beloved James Braid used to do this sort of thing till the day of his death when he was over eighty, but I cannot think of anybody else quite in the same class. At the same time some of our Seniors, who are, comparatively speaking, little boys in frilly petticoats compared with Michael Scott, have lately been doing great things.

Only last week I was writing about the bold Brigadier W. H. H. Aitken, who contributed so richly to the Society's victory over the Australians. To go out in 31 at Woking, and to be still three under fours after the seventeenth hole, despite two sixes, is far from despicable, even for a mere youth of fifty-five or so. Only a few days before he had halved for the Seniors' Championship with a rather more mature golfer, H. J. T. Neilson, aged sixty, with a score of 72 at St Andrews. He had also driven the home green on the Old Course, which the book tells me is 380 yards long. I think the newspapers called it a little less, 356 yards or so, but even that, as Mr Bob Acres might have remarked, 'is a good distance.' I have seen Cyril Tolley achieve it and one or two other people have done it also; Edward Blackwell hit the steps up to the clubhouse and that with a gutty ball, but still it is a highly respectable shot and, moreover, those other heroes were younger.

Then there is the now almost fabulous T. A. Torrance, who is sixty-three. He did not win that Seniors' Championship, but he is constantly winning scratch medals at St Andrews and Sandwich in young and strong company. There is no doubt that age will be served.

Some of these gallant old—no, not old but almost middle-aged—gentlemen will soon be approaching the best time of life for going round in the number of their own years. I have little doubt that Michael Scott has reached that brief but happy prime and goes round the Royal Jersey course in seventy-six or under with perfect ease; but the others are not yet, so to speak, quite ripe.

It is hard to say what is the best age for the purpose. Torrance might comparatively soon be reaching it, if he lived on a short course, but as most of his golf is played on the two great Sandwich courses of St George's and Princes, I hardly think he will do it just yet awhile. I don't suppose any man can hope to do it till he is nearing sixty-nine and then the time is short. I remember, a good many years ago a very pleasant old gentleman and a very keen golfer, Captain Reade, late RN, who achieved it at sixty-nine round Sudbrook Park. He was quite a good golfer, but by no stretch of imagination a great one, and charming Sudbrook was in those days—I fancy it is harder now—just the course for his purpose. I have a strong impression that Walter Blackwell went round Rye in sixty-eight when he had attained precisely that age and, if so, that was truly noteworthy, for Rye is no child's play for anybody.

There is one thing about these remarkable scores done by players past the first flush of youth which puzzles me, though perhaps it is only part of the general puzzle of lower and lower scores. Here are these old gentlemen—the phrase will out—who are doing lower scores now than they did when they were years and years younger. What is more, they often do lower scores than, let us say, Harry Vardon did round the very same courses. Now I am sure that they cannot be better players now when in their fifties or sixties than they were in their thirties, and, with all respect to them, I am still more sure that Vardon was a much better player than they ever were or will be. Yet there are the figures.

I know golf has improved. However much I stick up for the heroes of my youth, I have to admit that the chipping and putting of the best golfers has made great strides, and that this partially at any rate accounts for the scores in the higher circles. But when all is said there still remains, for me at least, some insoluble mystery. Granted the greater smoothness of courses, the longer flight of balls, the perfection of numbered sets of clubs—granted anything you like; I am still baffled. At any rate all these feats of the not-so-young must be immensely encouraging to their contemporaries, who need never give up hope. I am myself so much cheered by reading of my old friend in Jersey slaughtering insurgent youth that I am almost moved to take a club out once more into my field I am afraid it would hurt too much and the ball would not go, but it is tempting.

WITH A RED BALL
(1955)

I wonder whether the golfers of fifty or sixty years ago were more hardy or more foolish than those of today. I ask the question because it occurs to me that it is a long while since I saw a red golf ball and I think that in remote ages the professional generally had one or two in his shop, ready painted in case of lunatics' wanting to play in the snow. For many years I possessed one myself as a keepsake, but I have lost it long since. It was a gutty, and, though I may be talking nonsense, I do not remember ever to have seen a red rubber-cover. Was it not Andrew Kirkaldy who oiled his caddie's head so that he could casually rub his ball on the boy's hair and so prevent the snow from sticking to it? If people have ceased to play in the snow I am far from deeming them unwise. I cannot think it a good or even an amusing game. This is rather weather for practising putting on the carpet before a blazing, crackling fire.

My own recollections of golf with a red ball belong chiefly to my first year at Cambridge, because that was the year of the long frost when people could skate all the way to Ely. It began, as I remember, towards the end of January (an ominous thought at the time when I write) and went on into March. So nearly the whole of the Lent term the golf courses were snow-bound and hard as ice.

One of my random memories is of the beginning of the term when there was only a light covering of snow. Some other young gentlemen and I went to play at Worlington and I still hear the indignant voice of my opponent crying aloud, 'The blighter's tee'd it.' Well, I had certainly scraped away the snow behind the ball, so that it remained on an encouraging little eminence, but I am not convinced that I had done wrong. At any rate I took my brassie to the next shot.

Now for a gentle little boast. Am I now, I wonder, one of the few people alive who have won a scratch medal with a red ball? The Linskill Cup was our scratch prize played for once a term and we put the competition off and off, hoping for kinder conditions. Still there was no letting up of the weather and at last it was decreed that we must play. Coldham Common was white with snow, not deep but definite, and a small space was cleared round each hole. It was a very small space and one was likely to pitch one's ball over one little wall of snow and run across into that on the other side.

I remember clearly only one stroke—my first. The first hole was a one-shotter and being wholly out of practice, as we all were, I came very near to missing the globe. I said I had slipped; perhaps I really had; at any rate the ball, in the words of the rule, left its position and came to rest in another place, not very far off. I was thankful to get a five. I must have played better afterwards, for my score was 92. How good or how bad it was I cannot now say, but at least it was several strokes better than anyone else's. If the old funnel-shaped cover of leather stamped with golden names still encloses the Linskill Cup, my name and score will be found there to witness if I lie.

Red balls again played their part some three years later in a match of which I was only a spectator. This was the blizzard match between the two Universities at Sandwich in 1898, the year after I had gone down. I have, I am conscious, described before how the snowstorm came down suddenly out of a steely March sky, driving the players into the clubhouse, nearly all of them with their matches unfinished; how the stony-hearted and impartial Mr T. R. Mills from his warm sitting-room at the Bell decreed that they must go out again in the fast-gathering darkness to complete their rounds.

There were some red balls in Ramsay Hunter's shop, but not enough to go round, and those players had the better chance who hit the balls so short a distance as not to lose them. That was a policy that could be overdone, as by one player who twice played the ball on to his own boots. They were button boots, since he had prematurely changed, not expecting the cruel order to go out again.

I suppose there has been only one match deserving the epithet historic played in the snow, and that was a long time ago, in the winter of 1875. It was the last match played by young Tommy Morris a little while before his death, and there is a full account of it in *The Life of Tom Morris*. Arthur Molesworth, of the Westward Ho! family, a fine golfer in his day and an elder competitor of Horace Hutchinson on the Devon links, had issued a challenge to play any professional with the odds of a third, and Tommy had been persuaded to accept it. It was played for three days running at St Andrews, in bitter weather, and for most of the time the course was covered with snow. We are told that the umpire thought that the match should be postponed, but that the amateur insisted on playing. What were the exact conditions of the match and what the umpire's powers I do not know, but he does not seem to have been very resolute. Molesworth presumably thought that the snow would prove an equaliser, but he does not seem to have been right. The greens were swept, and Tommy could pitch on the frozen ground and make the ball stop, whereas his adversary could not. I imagine his doing it with his niblick, with which he was extraordinarily skilful, and pitching with an old niblick, with a face of about the size of half-a-crown (slightly larger than a 10p piece), demanded much skill; the very thought of the danger of socketing gives one a pain. At any rate, Tommy won easily, by 9 and 7 according to the *Badminton*. He was very unhappy after the death of his wife, and bored with the game, and went on only for the sake of his backers. It is hard to imagine a more thoroughly depressing affair and my goodness! how cold St Andrews can be if it tries.

I am not sure whether Braid ever played in the snow on bleak Walton Health, but I should not be at all surprised, for, monumentally calm as he appeared, there never was a keener and more passionately devoted golfer. When, after his death, I wrote a little book about him, his cousin and helper in the shop, Will Brown, told me a story about him which I venture to repeat. When there was so much snow on the ground that it was obviously out of the question to play, James would get restless and ill at ease. Evéry now and again he would leave the shop for a minute or two. Nobody said anything, but everybody knew that he had gone to look hopefully for any sign of a thaw that should soon make golf possible again.

After I had told that small story in the book, I had a letter from an old friend telling me how, years before, he and James had played a game together at Chiswick with the course covered with snow. That was when James was working at a West End stores and had only his Sundays to play on, so that he doubtless felt starved for golf and no snow could stop him.

There is just about one thing, and one thing only, to be said for snow from a golfing point of view: a seaside course never looks quite so perfect as when the snow has left it. It may be imagination, but it always seems to me as if the kind snow had gently stroked down each individual blade of grass, as if it were doing the course's hair for it for a party. And then it is such fun to see one's enemy's ball go into a dear little pot-bunker, where the snow has lingered, so that one knows he will not be able to get out. Or rather it used to be such fun, but now that the rule says snow and ice are casual water, one's demoniac glee will never be the same again. The confounded fellow will be able to pick it out for the loss of one wretched stroke. It was lovely when he had to hack and hack at it in vain.

BATTLE DRESS
(1956)

When I was at Deal and Sandwich for the Halford Hewitt
Cup the other day it occurred to me that the spectacle of
more than five hundred golfers of various ages and shapes
and sizes afforded an interesting study in the golfer's gar-
ments. What first put it into my head was searching the
horizon for the first Eton pair, and, catching sight of their
respective and eminently characteristic headgears, I found
myself repeating the lines that I had learnt in the schoolroom
from Macaulay's *Ivry*.

Press where you see my white plume shine, amidst the ranks of
> *war*
And be your oriflamme today the helmet of Navarre.

I had to misquote and make it a red plume to suit Philip
Scrutton's flaming red beret, which made a really admirable
oriflamme, and his partner, Dru Montagu, reinforced it by a
small but unmistakable blue hat of inexpressible jauntiness.
When I saw these two in the distance I knew that the
supreme moment of agony and triumph was approaching.

So many people today play hatless that these two crests
were the more striking. Of course there were some caps, but
it struck me that the era of magnificent checks was past.
There were, on the other hand, some striking hats. John

Beck, who needs it to keep the rain from his spectacles, had a fine old specimen with brim well turned down. There seemed to me something vaguely furtive about it, as of one desiring to avoid notice. George Duncan, of Rugby, on the other hand, had a hat suggesting a game of Cowboys and Indians, extremely picturesque. We had another beret on the Eton side, a black one, palpably sinister, worn by one of our admirable third pair, Turnbull. No doubt there were other notable examples, but for the most part I recall uncovered heads.

This matter of headgear is comparatively insignificant. The great and double change, since I first knew golf, is, of course, in the complete superseding of the coat by the woolly (I do not count waterproof coats) and the almost equally complete victory of trousers over knickerbockers. The coat has gone so long that it is missed, if at all, only by venerable persons. Yet when I think of the great amateurs of my youth it is impossible, nay it would be absurd, to picture them in anything but a jacket and knickerbockers. I have just looked yet again at my *Badminton* volume, not to verify my memories, but out of sentimental satisfaction. This is not my precious first edition, which has almost disintegrated and has to be tenderly handled, but a comparatively modern one dated 1902. Here they all are: Horace Hutchinson himself, the Editor, John Ball, Harold Hilton, Freddie Tait, Leslie Balfour, Robert Maxwell, and all coated and knicker-bockered cap-à-pie. And to my prejudiced eye, very well they look, with something of dignity that is lacking in their be-woollied and trousered successors, with very baggy knees.

I think it was the coming of the conquering American golfers after the first World War that convinced us that jerseys were better than coats. They looked so lithe and free,

and swung so easily. I have no doubt at all that the jersey or
pullover—call it what you will—is the better garment, but it
took some learning. I remember that when during that war I
played on Macedonian plains in a sweater or in summer
shirt-sleeves I acquired a nasty slice, but cured it at once on
coming home by putting on a nice tight coat. In fact, I think I
became truly accustomed to a woolly only when it did not
much matter what I wore. Such few very humble triumphs
as I ever enjoyed were won in a coat. Horace Hutchinson
wrote with commendation of 'the veteran shooting coat
which has taken colour from all kinds of wind and weather,
and clings adaptably in loving, familiar wrinkles to the
owner's frame.' My coats were always made of grey flannel
and were old and wrinkled enough. And let the wearers of
woollies remember in impotent envy that they had lots of
pockets.

Well, coats have gone for ever and nobody would really
want to see them back again; but I sometimes wish the habit
of knickerbockers might be revived. I preach what I do not
and indeed cannot practise, as my two remaining pair of
knickerbockers were devoured by the malignant moths
during the last war. Nor can I advance any particular reason
why they should be superior to trousers and they are more
trouble. Yet they did look on the whole smarter and tidier,
and they were at one time almost universal.

Here again I have been studying in my *Badminton* and
looking for a picture by Harry Furniss called *Understudies*.
From my earliest youth I had the good taste to think those
pictures very ugly and not the least amusing, and I cut all of
them that I could out of my own edition; but this particular
one has value as an historical document. It shows eight pairs
of legs from the knee downwards; six of the eight are in
one form or another knickerbockered and only two are

trousered. Three are likewise spatted, and there is quoted the complaint of some crusty old golfer that 'no one can play with his eye constantly caught by those confounded spats.'

I do not know what originally started the pendulum of fashion swinging so vigorously in favour of trousers; perhaps it was the appallingly exaggerated character of the plus-fours on the legs of young gentlemen who were, I imagine, to be seen on the front at Blackpool or Margate. That is only a guess, and perhaps a wrong one: I have been trying to think of any distinguished players who are faithful to the elder fashion and can recall only one for certain. He is certainly distinguished, for he is, perhaps, the best amateur golfer in Britain at the moment, David Blair, and he always looks as neat as a new pin. Of course, there must be others, but I cannot be sure of them.

I have been looking proudly at the photograph of the victorious Eton side in last week's *Country Life*, and they seem to be trousered to a man. And, after all, we are only going back to a still older fashion, as witnessed by the famous picture of the *Finish of a Great Match*, at St Andrews, with Sir David Baird, Sir Ralph Anstruther, Major Playfair and other worthies of a century or more ago. The players are wearing trousers and they are also wearing tall hats. Tall hats and knickerbockers would, I fear, never do.

THE TERRIBLE CHOICE
(1957)

I read with regret the other day of the death of an old golfing acquaintance whom I had not seen for many years. His name suddenly and vividly recalled to my mind a match we had once played together. It was hardly a match because we did not know which of us was up or down; we went out to cure each other's diseases. He was complaining of hooking his drives and I bemoaning a mild but temporarily incorrigible slice from the tee. Surely we should be able to help each other, but the round was not a success, for each of us, far from pitying the other's weakness, was bitterly envious of it; understanding was hopelessly imperfect.

He began with a fine long drive, as I should have called it, with a nice little turn to the left which just took it into some very innocent rough. 'There it goes again!' he exclaimed, and was furious when I said that, if that was all, he had no need to be sorry for himself; I wished I had only half his complaint. Then I hit my drive, on the fairway to be sure, but having a paltry, slicy air. When I broke into loud lamentations he declared that I ought to be thankful and that a slice was far less calamitous than a hook. We returned to the clubhouse after eleven holes, our attempts at mutual doctoring having failed miserably.

Thinking over that round again I recalled W. S. Gilbert's

famous lines, in the Sentry's song, declaring that every boy and every girl was born 'either a little Liberal or else a little Conservative.' I wondered whether we were all born hookers or slicers, and if so which was the more fortunate lot. Once upon a time I should have said that slicing was infinitely the worse of the two. I don't know that I was born either, and as a boy, if I may say so, I was rather a good driver, but in the middle of my first year at Cambridge I was suddenly stricken with an appalling attack of slicing. Perhaps no very good medical advice was at hand; at least, no one could cure me and for several years I was subject to periodical attacks. I remember one bout in a gale of wind at Westward Ho!, but even now the memory of my ball being swept into inaccessible rushes is too painful. In any case, my personal history is not interesting; enough then that in time I overcame the disease, but never, I think, quite overcame the fear of it, so that I lacked something of confidence in hitting ever afterwards.

Then it certainly seemed to me that to be a hooker was a blessing, and to be a slicer was a curse, and I am inclined to think that in those days of the gutty this was more or less true. The gutty was so light and could be such a helpless plaything for wind that blew on one's back; liability was utterly unlimited. The man who could hold the ball up into that wind seemed the most enviable of all mortals. To be sure, the hooker could also suffer from the opposite wind, but I decline to believe that his sufferings were so great. And then, of course, there was the question of length. Harold Hilton, who could do almost anything with the ball, deliberately cultivated a turn to the left to gain in distance of run. Moreover, there was something manly about a hook, even if it was occasionally disastrous, and a gentle feebleness about a slice. I was ashamed of mine.

Today things have considerably changed and I am by no means sure that the slicer is not the more to be envied. When I say 'slicer,' I ought to define my terms and say one whose ball is inclined to turn if anything to the right, so that he can hold the ball up into a right-hand wind. I suppose the class that swings 'from inside out' is pre-eminently one of hookers. Such a master of the art as Henry Cotton no doubt 'rides the whirlwind and directs the storm,' but I have seen others of the inside-out school who lack his mastery, so finding great difficulty in approaching the green in a right-to-left wind. If American golfers have any weakness, as to which I am by no means certain, it is this. It is probably owing to the fact that they do not habitually play in such strong winds as we do. Even the great Bobby Jones, I think, preferred to play his shot to the green in a right-hand wind with a curl from the right. Of course, he could do it with great skill, as he could everything, but he was a little lacking in the shot right up to the green in that wind's eye. Such, at least, is my possibly irreverent impression.

On the whole, I fancy that the hooker, when he errs, does go into deeper and more disastrous trouble than the slicer. I have quoted before, but it gives me pleasure to quote again, dear James Braid's joyously malignant remark as Densmore Shute hit a wild hook at Walton Heath: 'He'll want all his dynamiters there.' James himself, if ever he did make a crooked shot, inclined to hit it to the left, sometimes, though very rarely, into real dynamiter country. I remember a famous golfer, a contemporary of his, saying that, considering his great powers, Braid's record of five Championships and all the rest did not really do him justice, and this he attributed to that very occasional but expensive hook. What a wonderful compliment! I am not saying that he was right or wrong, but it is an interesting opinion of one well worth listening to.

For a hooker to be able to turn himself into a member of the other school for a particular occasion is a splendour of skill that very, very few could accomplish. When Harold Hilton came up to Prestwick for the Amateur Championship of 1911 he found the ground dry and burnt and fast as lightning. He had been habitually turning his drives from right to left for some years then and he found his tee-shots just ending in the left-hand rough, whereas Cecil Hutchison, his opponent in the international match, whose ball turned a little the other way, was safe on the fairway. He instantly set to work to recapture his old method of driving with a slight turn to the right. Length mattered little on that iron-hard ground, but straightness was all-important. He had not much time in which to make the reform, but he did it and he won that championship. He won another championship two years later, having reverted to the drive with his ever-artistic turn of hook.

When on the subject of reforming hookers, I must not forget perhaps the greatest of them all, Ben Hogan. He used to have a very occasional hook and he thought that it had cost him very dearly. No doubt he was right in the highly competitive company he frequented, when a single stroke might make all the difference. Then, as he has told us, an inspiration came to him in the watches of the night and he could hardly wait before dashing to the practice tee to try the remedy. It was a great success, but what it was he told nobody for a long time. When he did disclose this 'secret' it proved perhaps a little disappointing to those expecting some world-shaking revelation, since it consisted, if I remember rightly, only in a slightly increased opening of the face of the club.

Of course, such gross words as 'hook' and 'slice' ought really not to be used with regard to great men. I should rather have employed 'draw' and 'fade.' 'Draw' was the word that Hilton, I think, always used to describe his so beautifully controlled method of driving, when he was beginning to find he wanted a little more length. But for ordinary people I think that the old, cruder words are best. As I have said before, nobody knows what a slice could be unless he played with a gutty ball and a wooden shaft. The modern ball bores through the wind and the steel shaft does not leave the head behind as the wooden one used to do. I believe fading is today the art to be cultivated, but I cannot secretly help wishing I had been born a hooker. It is such a fine, virile vice. By the way, didn't J. H. once ask: 'What's the matter with the middle of the course?' There is something to be said for that, too.

NUMBER FIVE WOOD
(1958)

I am wondering whether wood is beginning to come back into a little of its old kingdom at the expense of the clanging armament of irons. It can only be to a small extent, but one certainly seems to hear more talk of the No. 4 wood and even the No. 5. Indeed, I read the other day a remark of Locke to the effect that the No. 2 iron had had its day, since it had been supplanted by the No. 5 wood. Today it is odd to reflect that once upon a time the wooden clubs in a golfer's so greatly outnumbered the irons. The picture called *Modern Golf Clubs* in a *Badminton* volume shows seven of wood and of iron only four. I recall that Horace Hutchinson was once asked by a friend to go to a picture-dealer's shop where there was an old golfing picture that he was minded to buy. Horace at once decided that the picture was a fraud, since at the alleged date the player would have had far more wooden clubs and fewer irons; so there was no deal.

Exactly what the date was supposed to be I do not remember, but the coming of iron clubs in any quantity is not so very long ago. Just over a hundred years ago was first published a charming little book, since reprinted, *The Golfer's Manual by a Keen Hand.* The author was in fact one Farnie, a well-known playwright in his day. Clearly he was in two minds as to the iron invaders. He sets out wooden clubs at some length, headed by the driver and going on to a whole family of spoons, long, middle, short and baffing. The niblick was likewise apparently of wood, 'an antiquated connection of the spoon family.' Of irons there were at most four—the bunker, the driving and the light iron, and the cleek or click. The author was a good conservative. He tried to be against these new-fangled weapons; he advised that on a medal day the player should 'give his iron clubs a holiday.' Yet he had to admit that, when it came to lofting over a bunker close to the green, the light iron was 'most useful.'

Gradually the irons won the day and all the family of spoons was cut down to a single one. There have always been great spoon players. Herd and Duncan are the names that come quickly to mind and very particularly, of course, Harold Hilton. He had when in doubt more confidence in a wooden club than an iron. When the Mills aluminium putter first appeared and enjoyed great popularity, the same firm made a series of aluminium spoons and baffies. Hilton used them for a while and that, needless to say, very skilfully. I do not recollect, however, that he had in that respect many imitators. One golfer, with whom at one time I played many rounds, the late W. E. Fairlie, generally called Tony and a member of a famous golfing family, was unique in using a battery of lofted wooden clubs. He was a very good player, a St Andrews medal-winner and a Scottish international. My recollection is that it was only when he came to quite short pitching shots that he used a mashie. Otherwise it was some variation of what *The Golfer's Manual* would have called the baffing spoon, and very deftly he used it.

When it comes to the modern No. 4 and No. 5 woods, I must admit to writing without any personal experience, because they have come into popularity since I had to give up playing. Yet I may hazard a view as to their merits. One is their shallowness. I have always thought that many golfers would do better with slightly shallower-faced clubs, since not only do they make it easier to pick up the ball, but they make it look easier, and certainly confidence is enormously important in playing wooden shots through the green.

Then again I imagine they make it less difficult to play the kind of shot with a fade, and particularly to hole up the ball into a right-hand wind. I must have quoted before Robert Maxwell's remark that if he wanted to judge a golfer he would watch him playing iron shots into a strong wind from the right. It is not a simple thing to do. In fact, so hard is it that many players give up the attempt and try to allow for the hook. That holding-up shot is, I feel sure, easier for most people to play with some sort of spoon, and that is one of the occasions when a No. 5 wood must come in useful. At least I think so, but I may not be talking such good sense as I fancy.

There is one thing that may safely be said on behalf of more or less lofted wooden clubs, namely that they do not take such divots as do the irons. Horace Hutchinson wrote of the Mills spoons that 'the aluminiums, with their flat soles, go on over the ground after it is struck and do not stick in it or stay there as the irons do.' Indeed, the name of the old baffing spoon denoted its chief quality, since to baff, according to the glossary, means 'to strike the ground with the sole of the club-head in playing and to send the ball in the air.' Such clubs are the greenkeepers' friends. There is a consequence of divots as to which I feel rather bitterly, though it is on other people's behalf and not my own. I believe it is largely the effect of frenzied divot-takers that golfers are now driven to unengaging practice grounds, whereas once upon a time it was perfectly licit to practise on the course.

This certainly is so on one course in which I take an

interest. There the villains of the piece used to put down a dozen or so of balls in a row and hit them one after another with a No. 2 or No. 3 iron, leaving as a result a row of gaping wounds. When they have repeated this process several times, they have made a desert of what was once a smiling stretch of turf. Doubtless they do it with the best intentions, obeying the advice of those who tell them how Hogan and other great men have practised for several hours a day. But in consequence of this violence of virtue, poor harmless persons who like to take out a club in the cool of the evening and play a shot or two as the spirit moves them are driven away by authority and must go and disport themselves in a muddy and unattractive field. If I were still a golfer I should in this case be a defiant and persistent law-breaker.

'Were I as thou,' said the Black Knight to the jovial Friar (in *Ivanhoe*), 'I would take my walks by moonlight, when foresters and keepers were warm in bed, and ever and anon—as I pattered my prayers—I could let fly a shaft among the herds of dun deer that feed in the glades.' So I should wander down some secret valley and ever and anon I let fly my ball, when the fierce eyes of the secretary could not spy me. That is, I should do such a thing if I could play and if I were not on the committee. As it is, I hope that some other lawless spirits occasionally do so. I undertake to turn the blindest of eyes to the telescope if I see them at it.

I am afraid this vicarious grievance of mine has taken me far away from my original topic, but when I think of the happy times I have spent in practising on many famous and beloved courses till the dusk fell and the lights came out twinkling in the houses, I incline to see red. I hate the place that the Americans call the practice tee (why tee?). In fact, I am no doubt thoroughly unreasonable.

BARGAINS ON THE GREEN
(1959)

There was a good deal of comment provoked the other day by the bargain struck by two players in a thirty-six-hole match of considerable importance. With a single hole to go, after a close and magnificent struggle, they agreed to call the last hole, and so the match, a half, and the crowd were rather taken aback by the sight of the two players picking up their balls when neither could by the wildest stretch of imagination be termed dead. I am not going to praise their 'chivalry' or condemn their 'flippancy,' to employ two terms applied to their bargain. I think that, however well intentioned, it was a mistake and had better not have been made, and with that I shall let the matter rest. It does, however, open up the general question of such agreements and of the morality or otherwise of offering a half, whether of a hole or a match.

I am reminded of an ancient verse to be found, I think, in Clark's *Golf, a Royal and Ancient Game*:

> *'Halved hole,' says the foe, but 'No' I say 'No';*
> *Putt it out, mine enemie!*
> *You're dead but not buried? He's shaky and flurried!*
> *Oh! a terrible miss makes he.*

It is a rare occurrence when the offer of a half is declined. The man to whom it is offered is placed in rather an invidious position, especially if, as in the case in question, he is the younger and less distinguished player of the two. He does not like to be unfriendly and further he cannot help feeling that he will look a fool should he be the one to miss. Indeed, I can remember seeing the thing happen only once, in a University match a good long time ago. The Cambridge man, who was, I think, one up with four to play, offered a half of the fifteenth hole and the Oxford man resolutely but politely declined. Thereupon Cambridge missed, Oxford holed and in the end Oxford won the match. I dimly remember, though I was not there, that something of the same sort happened in a match between J. H. Taylor and Andrew Kirkaldy in the now almost prehistoric ages; at least Andrew said so in his book of reminiscences, but who holed and who missed I have forgotten. I fancy Andrew must have had the better of it, or he would not have remembered it quite so well.

No doubt it would have been better if the habit of giving putts or taking halves had never come into existence and we all had solemnly to hole out whatever the circumstances. But human nature is too strong for us, and after all it would be absurd to refuse a man the right of giving up the hole. I remember once in Macedonia playing a foursome in a match between a depot and a hospital in which I had my own much-loved general as my partner. On the first green our adversaries, out of respect perhaps to his rank, wanted to give him a putt for the half. He resolutely declined the offer and then missed the putt, at which I showed, I fear, some ill-disciplined dissatisfaction. I don't think we ever quite recovered from the blow; at any rate we lost, and after some forty years nothing has altered my view that if you are given a putt, however foolishly, you had better accept it.

It is the giving of putts that is a mistake, and produces the grievance of not being given one and the utterly unjustifiable expectation of a *quid pro quo* in the matter of putts given. 'I should not do that if I were you,' said a well-known international, an old friend of mine now dead, to a young opponent who gave him a missable putt on the first green. 'If you have a putt like that to hole towards the end of the match, I shan't give it to you.' It was a wise and kindly-meant warning against the hope of reciprocal favours, and no doubt as a close match gets nearer and nearer to its finish, so the length of the putts conceded palpably diminishes. I remember hearing Francis Ouimet advise someone never to give an opponent a putt for the match, however short, and there is no doubt at all it is good advice. The final moment on the very edge of victory can sometimes be strangely unnerving.

How long is the shortest putt ever missed? And by that I mean missed by a man trying seriously to hole it, not by somebody who hits the ball one-handed with the back of his putter. It is a question that cannot be answered, but there have been cases of putts solemnly measured and found to have been nine inches long. There was one missed by Mr Leslie Balfour Melville which that solemn student of the game, Mr Everard, vowed and declared to be just over seven inches. I remember that at the first championship in which I took part, at Hoylake, now 61 years ago, Freddie Tait beat Jack Graham, then a great local hero second only to Ball and Hilton, at the last hole, and Jack was said to have missed the very shortest of all known putts. I did not see it, but after tea I saw all the little boys of Hoylake practising what was alleged to be the putt. Possibly it had by that time a little diminished: certainly the little boys were holing it with the greatest dash and confidence and it looked well under a foot in length.

It is only human nature to like to be given a short putt on the first green, but it is far better to have to put it in. The cheerful sound of a short one holed is most reviving to the spirits, and, if it so happens that we do not have to get one in till several holes have been played, the inevitable moment when it comes is the more unpleasant. That is one of few charms of score play: the horrid process of holing out is not postponed but must be faced at once. I have known cunning players who, when their adversary has two for it on the first green, immediately give him the hole with a lofty gesture. This is not done from excessive generosity, far from it: the giver thinks that he would hole it anyhow and in doing it would gain a knowledge of the pace of the greens. I do not uphold this as an example to be followed; it is unattractively crafty, even though it may not quite amount to puttmanship.

An example of genuine and detestable puttmanship comes back to me from a championship of past years. On the last green A was left with a putt of perhaps two and a half for the match, whereupon B remarked: 'I wish I could give you that one, but I'm afraid I ought to ask you to hole it.' Thereupon B duly missed the putt and lost the match at the nineteenth. The rule of conduct is of course perfectly clear. If you do not mean to give your enemy the putt (there is no reason why you should), you must stand as silent as a statue and let him putt. Even too long a consideration of the putt is to be deprecated and is as suggestive as too long a consideration of a hand before declaring at bridge. What a lot of trouble and heartburning would be saved if we holed every putt as a matter of course, but if there is one thing in the world entirely certain it is that we never shall.

THE DEPARTED CLEEK
(1960)

I suppose we all amuse ourselves at times by deciding, if the power of summoning up some scenes from the past were given to us, on what particular event in history our choice would fall. We might choose Alfred letting the cakes burn, or we might, should our interest be in murders, like to solve the Balham mystery by seeing who put the antimony in poor Mr Bravo's water-jug, or was it in his bottle of Burgundy? I have played this game by myself very often and fancied what fun it would be to see the Grace family, with W.G. as a little boy, playing their game of family cricket in the orchard at Downend.

Of course I have done it often with scenes from old golf, and there is one in particular that I should dearly love to recall from the past. It is recorded that some time in the 1870s young Tommy Morris and Bob Ferguson played a match at St Andrews, each being armed only with a cleek, and Bob Ferguson won. I believe that match would be a liberal education to watch in the matter of improvising shots. The cleek was then a favourite maid-of-all-work: both would be equally skilled at playing pitch-and-run or running-up shots with it.

Likewise men used to putt with their driving cleeks now and then, if the green was rough or the ball lay badly, and so both men would be well prepared there, but the short chips and pitching shots over bunkers would be eminently testing, and I am sure they would surprise us with their skill. The modern player, if he had to play such a match, would choose, I presume, a No. 3 iron and doubtless he would be very skilful with it, given a little practice, but a man who has to worry his brains as to whether to use a No. 8 or No. 9 might find himself a little at sea with that one comparatively straightforward club.

Needless to say, he never will have to, because matches of that sort are seldom if ever made nowadays. I wish to goodness they were. I would rather a hundred times watch one than the endless processions of score play round rather dull park courses. I shall never get the chance, however, and indeed matches have clean gone out of fashion. When was the last gauntlet thrown down and picked up between professional golfers? A sadly long time ago. Nobody is to blame; it is simply that there is more money to be made at these weary tournaments, and they want more of them still.

For that matter, I don't think amateurs indulge in such amusements as one-club matches as much as they used to. It was the kind of game that used to be played late on a summer evening, and very good fun it was, with modest wagering upon the results. Hoylake in its early days was the scene of entertaining matches, played by moonlight or in a thick fog or what not. It was a Hoylake golfer who won, I believe, very considerable bets at Pau by going round with a putter alone. This was Mr Charles Hutchings, who won the Amateur Championship at the age of fifty-three. His putter, a Parks crook-necked club, was well suited to the purpose, for it had a particularly long shaft and he often used it instead of a driving iron through the green. I believe he began by betting he would go round in 90 with his putter; then he reduced the figure and the odds against him naturally grew longer. Finally he finished in 80. My figures may not be quite accurate, but they are not far out, I believe. Pau in those days was full of sporting characters and I expect a good deal of money changed hands. As I remember the course, it is flat and there would be no great demand for much lofted shots.

Generally speaking, it is dangerous to bet against the man armed only with a putter. He generally knows a good deal about his one weapon. I remember Mr 'Boxer' Cannon hitting prodigious shots with his putting cleek round Worlington. If putter meant only the old wooden club, as it once did, it would be a different matter. Incidentally, some years ago there was a considerable dispute at a course near London about a match in which one player undertook to play another when armed only with his niblick, or I suppose it was his No. 9. It was alleged that he had had his niblick hammered up in the shop, whereby it became considerably less lofted and so capable of much greater length. That would doubtless have been deemed a proper proceeding in the days of, let us say, George Osbaldeston, when the great thing to do with a match was to win it and the great thing to do with a cat was not to let it out of the bag; but we have grown rather more particular in these days.

Thinking over the countless players I have known, I should certainly back Mr John Ball in a cleek match. Not only had he great power with it, but he had a remarkable gift of being able to play a lofted shot with a fairly straight-faced iron. He regularly used a mid-iron where other people would use a mashie and would even take it in a bunker. He had the gift—I don't know how he did it—of raising the ball quickly and high into the air with a club not apparently adopted to the purpose. The only final he ever lost in the Amateur Championship was on the nineteenth hole at St

Andrews against Mr Leslie Balfour Melville, when he took a mashie, to which he was unaccustomed, to play his pitch over the burn and pitched in instead.

I remember winning the first scratch medal I ever did win, aged fifteen I believe, when driving with a cleek, for the reason that I had broken my driver, not in a temper I may add, and could not get another. It was hard work and my score was atrocious; I don't know what the other players can have been about. It was a good cleek made by Mr Forrester of Elie, I think, and it was a sore grief when somehow or other I lost it. I cannot help thinking that it is a pity that the cleek has vanished from the earth, for it was a pleasant club and could make very pleasant shots. I suppose the No. 3 or No. 2 iron corresponds to it, but there was a wonderful sweetness about a good cleek shot that it seems to me the modern club cannot quite produce. However, perhaps I am only praising time past.

People used to have a club called an approaching cleek, with a shallow face like a driving cleek but, of course, more lofted. It became known by the vulgar name of jigger and gradually disappeared with the numbering of irons. The last player I remember using a club that was called a cleek was Mr de Montmorency. He called it, I think, with an affectionate diminutive, his little cleek, and it was rather short in the shaft, but he could hit the ball a long way with it. I seem to see him playing his tee shot to the old eighth hole at Rye (it is now the fifth) with it, and the ball going straight as an arrow through the wind.

STORMY WEATHER
(1961)

Sitting at home listening to the rain pattering on the window and waiting for news from Birkdale, I recalled other championships put off or nearly put off owing to rain. And I must begin by sympathising with the Royal Birkdale Club. There is no club, I think, more conscious of the honour of housing the Championship; no club of which the members more energetically combine to undertake all manner of necessary duties. The weather was very hard on them, and it was at least comforting that the conditions improved on the last day and the course emerged triumphant, as a fine test of golf.

I read that we have to go back to 1910 for an instance of the Championship being washed out as it was on the second day at Birkdale. Well, I can go back to the year 1910, at St Andrews, and a memorable one it was. One is apt to remember small ways in which one was oneself affected, and that storm of rain prevented me from going to Dornoch. It upset my plans, and in fact I have never seen Dornoch, a sad gap in my education. Then I remember going out in a downpour to see Willie Park. I had met him but never seen him play, and now here he was playing the first hole. He successfully reached the green in two and took two putts with his wrynecked putter, which he made so famous, and then came the announcement that the day's play was washed out and abandoned.

Some way in front was James Braid, in his policeman's mackintosh trousers, no longer of Romford but of Walton Heath. The message reached him, but presumably in rather a vague form. At any rate, he did not wholly believe it, deeming it too unofficial, and so went on ploughing his way through the rain-gushes. It must gradually have dawned on him that the news had been true, but, having once set on his voyage he continued and finished in 77 or 78, I think 78. It was a magnificent piece of golf in the conditions; one of the great rounds that do not count, which champions so often produce. Next morning, when he had to start again, he returned the very same score, and it seemed just about as good, though the rain had stopped.

Another famous stormy year was 1937, Cotton's year at Carnoustie. It was the last day of the Championship, as vile a day as could well be imagined, with a tempestuous wind and sheets of rain. It was obvious that there would be a grave danger of a wash-out. The first hole at Carnoustie is in a considerable hollow, which was sure to get full of water, and the green-keepers were kept busy cutting a fresh hole there, moving it ever further out of the hollow and up the bank. There were other greens, too, in great peril, and I have always had the feeling that, if anyone had protested, the day's play would have had to be abandoned. However, nobody did protest; I suppose they thought it was the same for all and they had had their chance; at any rate, they refrained from complaint is a very sporting manner, and the day's play was carried through somehow. I remember going out for a few holes with Reg Whitcombe at the very height of the storm and marvelling at him, thinking that nobody could possibly play better; yet Cotton, with the tempest but little abated, did play better and gained half-a-dozen strokes on him in the last two rounds. One of the most vivid pictures in my memory is of Whitcombe trying to shelter under his umbrella while he wiped his hands and the grip of his brassie on a towel, before playing his second to the home hole and then lashing the ball home over the burn and on to the green.

The alarming thing about these storms is that the flooding of a single green may wreck the whole day's play, and it is sometimes the green that one least expects. I remember one year at Sandwich when there came a sudden squall that nearly ruined everything. I had taken shelter with Cecil Hutchison, who was then a member of the Championship Committee, in the greenkeeper's tool-shed close to the eighth green. There we had a view of the seventh green, as innocent a green as possible, so one would imagine. But it has little ripples in it and in one of those little valleys the hole was cut. The valley quickly became full of water, and a couple came up who could not hole out. Cecil rushed out to summon the greenkeeping forces, and mobilised them with squeegees to sweep the water off the green. This they did, and the waiting couples, for there were more than one by this time, could go ahead and hole out. It would have been truly dreadful if that one little flood had destroyed a whole day's play, but that is the sort of thing that can happen. I remember, on that day at Carnoustie that I mentioned, a frantic message coming back to the Committee that a famous player refused to go on, and officials had to run out and pacify him and cut a fresh hole.

To return to Sandwich; it was the scene of a celebrated storm in, I think, 1938. It was not a storm of rain this time, but such a wind as I had never felt before. It blew down all the tents in the night and blew a good deal of money into the fortunate pockets of those who had backed the higher scores in a game, which I never fully understood, played on the Stock Exchange. The weather had been perfectly fine and easy for scoring and the scores had been very low accordingly; then came the tempest and they were blown to smithereens. I remember being quite unable to guess what sort of scores people could or would do. I went out with a friend to the ninth green to meet Whitcombe and Adams, who were playing together, wondering what we should hear. To our amazement we heard that Whitcombe was all fours and Adams very little worse. It is true that Whitcombe managed to take six to that hole by some ping-pong across the green; but even so he was out, unless my memory has gone astray, in 38, and the red book tells me his score for this third round was 75, truly miraculous in the circumstances. The wind really was tremendous: witness the fact that Padgham drove on to the eleventh green, where he rubbed it in by holing his putt for a two.

It seemed as if Cotton was going to do the most incredible score of all in the afternoon when he set out in pursuit of Whitcombe and Adams. It looked a hopeless business, but he played so supremely well that for fourteen holes it really seemed that he might do it. And then his iron shot up to the fifteenth hole was carried away over the little bank to the left of the green, and that meant a five. He could afford no more slips, and the sixteenth did it. I can still see his ball hovering high over the green before being swept into the left-hand bunker; the great spurt had been blown away.

The result of watching these tremendous events is, as far as I am concerned, a conviction that it is a mistake to believe that any storm will really defeat a great golfer; he will fight his way through it somehow. It will beat nearly all the field, but not quite all. The truly great ones will conquer, and it is unwise to bet against them.